T0290041

Learning and Researching with Case Studies

This companion takes the student through the different approaches to working with cases in the classroom, virtually and for research purposes. Capturing insights and best practices shared by scholars of the case method from around the world, this book aims to:

- equip students to work with and analyse case studies as part of their programme of study;
- adapt student approaches to online learning with cases;
- guide students on how to use case studies as a form of assessment;
- help students looking to adopt a case study approach to a research project.

These aims are framed in the sections of the book. Each section contains reflections from academics across the world, personal insights and lessons learnt from case sessions, templates, and exercises to develop your own skills in learning or researching with cases. Full examples showcase the nature of cases by type and format: short incident, exercise case, situation case; single, sequential and digital cases.

This text is for undergraduate and postgraduate Business and Management students, those studying as part of executive education programmes, MBA students, and academics who are using or preparing to use case studies in their learning or research. Online resources include PowerPoint slides, video material and example case studies from around the world.

Scott Andrews is a Principal Lecturer in Leadership and Business at the University of Worcester, UK. He is an experienced case study teacher and writer, having delivered more than 150 case development programmes across more than 30 countries. He is also a regular case user with undergraduates and postgraduates in his classes. Scott's cases have been adopted by business schools from across the world. He was appointed a Senior Fellow of the Higher Education Academy in recognition of his contribution to the global development of the case method.

Learning and Researching with Case Studies

A Student Companion for Business and Management Research

Scott Andrews

Routledge
Taylor & Francis Group

LONDON AND NEW YORK

Designed cover image: HAKINMHAN

First published 2024
by Routledge
4 Park Square, Milton Park, Abingdon, Oxon OX14 4RN

and by Routledge
605 Third Avenue, New York, NY 10158

Routledge is an imprint of the Taylor & Francis Group, an informa business

© 2024 Scott Andrews

The right of Scott Andrews to be identified as author of this work has been asserted
in accordance with sections 77 and 78 of the Copyright, Designs and Patents Act 1988.

All rights reserved. No part of this book may be reprinted or reproduced or utilised
in any form or by any electronic, mechanical, or other means, now known or
hereafter invented, including photocopying and recording, or in any information
storage or retrieval system, without permission in writing from the publishers.

Trademark notice: Product or corporate names may be trademarks or registered trademarks,
and are used only for identification and explanation without intent to infringe.

British Library Cataloguing-in-Publication Data
A catalogue record for this book is available from the British Library

Library of Congress Cataloging-in-Publication Data
Names: Andrews, Scott, 1970– author.
Title: Learning and researching with case studies : a student companion for
business and management research / Scott Andrews.
Description: Abingdon, Oxon ; New York, NY : Routledge, 2024. |
Includes bibliographical references and index. |
Identifiers: LCCN 2023014615 (print) | LCCN 2023014616 (ebook) |
ISBN 9781032386331 (hardback) | ISBN 9781032386324 (paperback) |
ISBN 9781003345978 (ebook)
Subjects: LCSH: Management–Research–Methodology. |
Management–Case studies. | Business–Research–Methodology. |
Business–Case studies. | Case method.
Classification: LCC HD30.4 .A596 2024 (print) |
LCC HD30.4 (ebook) | DDC 650.072–dc23/eng/20230330
LC record available at https://lccn.loc.gov/2023014615
LC ebook record available at https://lccn.loc.gov/2023014616

ISBN: 978-1-032-38633-1 (hbk)
ISBN: 978-1-032-38632-4 (pbk)
ISBN: 978-1-003-34597-8 (ebk)

DOI: 10.4324/9781003345978

Typeset in Berling and Futura
by Newgen Publishing UK

Access the Support Material: www.routledge.com/9781032386324

To Martha Hope

Who reminds me every day, what learning is really all about.

Contents

Figures

Foreword

As CEO of The Case Centre, I lead an organisation dedicated to supporting the acceptance, growth and development of the case method, one of the most powerful pedagogical learning approaches used with business and management students.

We've achieved a lot in our 50 years serving the case method community, and we now support educators and students at business schools and universities across the world. We distribute the world's most diverse case collection, curate the annual #WorldCaseTeachingDay, provide resources and support to case practitioners and students, and offer professional development pathways in case teaching and case writing.

Most importantly, the case method is a tool that increases student engagement, makes learning flourish, and helps to create successful future business leaders. Students learn to challenge assumptions, overcome prejudices, test theories, debate solutions and develop work and life skills – all critical skills to enhance employability.

However, learning with cases can be a challenging experience, and this book by Scott Andrews is exactly the type of resource needed to assist students.

Scott is a committed and experienced case scholar, and what makes this book stand out is that students don't only profit from Scott's invaluable insight, but from those of colleagues from across the globe who boast many years of working in case classrooms. Having access to such varied knowledge has never been more important as the case method continues to evolve, whether for in-class, virtual or research purposes. There are a myriad of experiences in different settings to share.

Scott is highly respected in the case method world, and I have seen him relay his extensive case method acumen when leading workshops on the practice at schools and conferences over many years. I know how much his input is valued by participants and have seen them growing in confidence and dexterity over the course of a workshop. You are in safe hands.

Scott also provided unique insight into the case instructor's viewpoint in our online resource for students, *Learning with Cases: An Interactive Study Guide*. The guide takes students through the process and Scott provides practical tips, tricks and tools about cases and the case method. Students learn how to analyse a case quickly and thoroughly using our practical Analysis Framework, prepare efficiently for class, participate in a case discussion, and plan for assessment through cases. Visit www.thecasecentre.org/LWCISG for more information.

I know you will find this companion essential reading and I hope that it supports you on your journey of learning to become a future business leader. I wish you success and enjoyment whist learning with the case method.

Vicky Lester
CEO, The Case Centre: the independent home of the case method
www.thecasecentre.org

Acknowledgements

This is my second book on the case method and is produced for all those students and scholars that I have had the privilege to meet in the case classroom over the past 28 years. *Learning and Researching with Case Studies: A Student Companion for Business and Management Research* is for you and for your contemporaries. It is for all students of management with a thirst for learning, a willingness to participate in the classroom, and a desire to immerse themselves in the stories captured in case studies. This book accompanies what I consider to be a sister book, *The Case Study Companion*, which was first published in 2021 to provide a resource for case study tutors, professors and facilitators. Neither book would have been made possible without the many years of friendship and support from the whole team at The Case Centre, and especially with Vicky, Richard, Kate, Hazel, Antoinette, Hannah, Lizzy and Gemma.

My thanks are extended to those case writers and scholars who kindly permitted me to use their material for this manuscript including Nazli Wasti, Burçak Ozoglu, J. David M. Wood, Michiel R. Leenders, Louise A. Mauffette-Leenders, James A. Erskine, Mark Saunders, Philip Lewis, Adrian Thornhill, Ronny Reinhardt, Sebastian Gurtner, Abbie Griffin, Stefi Barna, Emma Pencheon, Aditya Vyas, John Phillimore and Alan Tapper.

I am once again hugely grateful to the editorial team at Routledge who persevered with me throughout the drafting of the manuscript and supported its production, as well as the love, support, inspiration and ongoing encouragements from Rachel, Harry, Lois, Esme and Martha, and my colleagues from Worcester Business School, University of Worcester.

Introduction

The case study is more than 100 years old. Harvard published its first book of case studies in 1921[1] and ever since the case method has been widely used in university business schools and management centres around the world. You are probably reading this because you have been given the task of preparing for a case study as part of your own business or management course and, if so, then you join a longstanding and well-established academy of case scholars. This book sets out what the *case method* (or the *case study*, or simply the *case*) is all about and how you can make best use of it in your own programme, whether that is as a student preparing for a case discussion in class, studying to prepare your own case study assignment or conducting research using a case study approach. You will find plenty of insights and examples in this book to help you to make the most of the case method as a tool for learning and research.

This introduction sets the context for the book, helping you to understand what is meant by a case study, its origins and how it has been adapted over the past 100 years for use by a much wider global audience in contrast to its original postgraduate Harvard origins. It also sets out to explain the structure of the remainder of this book. It is for this reason that the book includes quotes from case scholars from around the world, to many of which I have identified the country of origin to showcase the diversity of creative thinking about the case method. These quotes demonstrate how the case has been adapted by many different cultures and for different learning environments.

The case study is now used by management scholars, lecturers and professors in business programmes around the world and has developed a proven track record to help you, the student, to not only look at how to solve problems, but also to develop a whole array of life skills that you can take back to your real world once the case session is over. For example, when you are preparing for a case class discussion, it is not so much about what you discover about the company under investigation in the case that really counts, but rather it's your ability to take the learning from this experience (often referred to as the 'takeaways') and apply them into other contexts. When we think about human muscle development, we recognise that the more you use it, the more it grows and develops. So, too, the more you practise your learning through the case method the more your own knowledge, skills and professional behaviours develop to prepare you for the next steps of your journey into business and management. In other words, as you immerse yourself in the case method, you start to see many sides to yourself that you can use to develop your own abilities in your future workplace. We often refer to these as *employability skills* and these are highly sought after by employers, often over and above basic knowledge acquisition.

DOI: 10.4324/9781003345978-1

To help you navigate your way through this book, each section has been broken down to focus on how the case method is used in different contexts. You could consider this like a buffet that you can keep returning to. You might not wish to start with the first chapter (although it's not a bad idea!), but you may wish to return to different parts of the book on different occasions depending on what you are being required to undertake as part of your course.

If you are totally new to the case concept, then Chapter 1 is a good place to start as it sets out in some detail what a case study really is all about and begins to explain how case studies can best be used to enhance your learning. The following chapters of this first section take you through a step-by-step guide to preparing for a case study in a classroom discussion, normally working with your peers and being led by a tutor or case facilitator. While the case has been adapted in many different cultural contexts and your tutors will no doubt adopt a range of different facilitating styles, there are some really helpful 'guiding principles' for preparation which, if put into practice, will undoubtedly help you to make the most of each case experience.

The case method had been adapted as a tool for online learning long before the Covid-19 pandemic forced business schools and management centres to switch their programmes to online delivery, so there are significant resources available to help you to consider how best to adapt to the case method for online programmes. This theme is developed further in the second section of this book, which looks at real-time (synchronous) online case classes and using cases for distance learning over a longer time period (adopting asynchronous delivery methods) and guides you to better anticipate the types of approaches that might be adopted by your tutors for this type of virtual learning environment.

It is perhaps not surprising that when your tutor adopts the case method as part of their teaching approach, then they are likely to use case studies for assessment and examination purposes too. So, the third part of this book looks at how you can best prepare for a case exam or to develop your own case study as a *case assignment*.

Following its successful implementation as a teaching tool in the classroom, there has more recently been a growth in the adoption of the case method as a qualitative research tool. This approach to research, which continues to be adapted and developed, is explored further in the fourth section of this book, which moves on from how we learn with cases in the classroom to how we can learn about management through case-based research, including some helpful tips to ensure you develop a clear and rigorous justification for your research approach.

The final section of this book signposts you to the many different organisations and resources from around the world that you can explore further to enhance your knowledge and awareness of the case method.

To help along the way, there are many examples cited from practice and a range of different case illustrations incorporated into this book to help you apply your thinking as you work through each section. All of the cases included in this book are also available at The Case Centre (www.TheCaseCentre.org), which has offices in the UK and US, and which holds the world's largest collection of management case studies. It is because of this that The Case Centre is frequently used within the text as a reference point for showcasing normal or good practice. When I first started out as a lecturer using case studies in my own classes, my mentor provided some invaluable insights. He would often refer to himself not so much as a lecturer or tutor but rather as a "learning facilitator on a voyage of discovery." For more than 30 years since those days, I have found myself on my own journey of discovery with the case method and have been fascinated to see how it has been used to support tens of thousands of management students around the world. I hope you find this a helpful and informative read and I wish you well as you continue your journey of discovery with the case method.

NOTE

1   Heath, 2015.

SECTION A

My Learning with Cases

Each of the five sections of this book focuses on a distinctive element of the case study method. In this first section, we look together at the use of case studies (or cases) in the classroom for case discussion. The moment your tutor places a case study in your hand (or emails you a case) with the instructions to prepare this case study for class discussion, you are invited to play your part in the active participant-centred learning process with which the case method has become so closely associated. But how do you do this and make the most of your time? And how do you ensure that you derive as much learning as you can from each in-class case experience? This section explores how to prepare for a class discussion, how to analyse cases studies and how to make the most of each different type of case that you may encounter on your course. The first chapter introduces your role as the case detective and then the next chapter includes a full case study with worked-out responses to help you consider how you could adopt a similar approach for a future case class discussion. More full case studies are included in subsequent chapters that consider not only how to work with paper (or pdf) cases but also how to engage with interactive digital cases, video and live case study sessions.

DOI: 10.4324/9781003345978-2

CHAPTER 1

What Are Case Studies and Why Are They Used for Learning?

This first chapter considers how the case study (or case) fits into your wider course or programme as one of many classroom approaches that your lecturers or professors might adopt. It explores how universities and colleges use cases as one tool in the class tutor's toolkit of learning resources. It provides information to explain the four processes of experiential learning you are likely to go through when using the case method and explores the role that you should take as a case participant to ensure the case session genuinely contributes to your learning and development.

But first, let's see what other people from around the world have to say about the reasons they use the case method:

> Case instructors facilitate discussion, asking lots of questions, writing comments on the board, and making occasional remarks. Students respond to questions, build on each other's comments, disagree with one another, ask questions, and try out different points of view about the case situation.
>
> (Harvard, US, 2018[1])

> For me, cases lie at the heart of the teaching process... A great case leads to great classroom dialogue and that leads to learning.
>
> (IMD, Switzerland, 2013[2])

> The case method is a powerful approach to teaching and learning business subjects. Its main advantage is that it is a "question-oriented," as opposed to "solution-based," approach to teaching. It allows students to participate in "real-life" decision making processes.
>
> (University of Hong Kong, 2004[3])

> Case and problem-based teaching methods [are] now primary modes of teaching in many leadership development programs because they offer situated learning and the means to try out multiple perspectives. In short, the approach provides professional development opportunities that are dynamic and grounded in "real-life" experiences.
>
> (University of Queensland, Australia, 2008[4])

DOI: 10.4324/9781003345978-3

1.1 THE CASE DETECTIVE

My Dad was a detective. He worked for the police and during my childhood he was frequently away conducting assignments. When I asked him what it meant to be a detective, his response would frequently be that he "solved cases." It is not surprising therefore that a common view of the case study is that it contains a 'problem' that needs to be 'solved'. However, the case study can be about far more than simply problem-solving. While different tutors have customised their view of the case method, no matter where you find yourself working with cases, you will undoubtedly be looking at a 'story' of an 'organisation' or a 'business'. Very occasionally the case might be about more than one business, a collection of organisations that together form one specific sector, or a group of businesses that are located within one single geographical region. That case study 'story' will contain data and, as the case detective, you will be expected to undertake some form of *review*, *analysis* or *investigation* into that data to make *inferences*, *decisions* or *recommendations*. You might be asked to metaphorically 'step into the shoes' of one the 'actors' in the case or to take a different view that allows you to evaluate the situation facing the organisation from an outsider perspective. For example, you might be asked to imagine you are a management consultant called in to advise the business.

As your analysis becomes informed by the story, your detective role will require you to work through the data contained within the case, and where appropriate to locate and investigate further data from outside of the case study too, in order to address a set of issues, questions or challenges. Often the story is based on a real situation within an organisation, although sometimes names, dates or locations may have been changed at the request of the organisation during the case-writing process to provide anonymity where needed. Sometimes, your tutor may be in possession of further information provided in addition to that contained within the case, in a tutor's note, to enhance their understanding of how to facilitate the discussion process and occasionally this might include details about 'what happened next'.

When you are first given the case study there are a number of things you could do to help in your preparation before the case is discussed in class. It's an old cliché: the more you put in, the more you get out; and this is certainly true when working with case studies. The preparation process might take considerably longer than the actual class discussion, but this all contributes to your overall learning, so no minute is a wasted minute.

One of the early Harvard pioneers of the case method was Professor Malcolm McNair, and this is what he had to say about the case study:

> A case study is a distinct literary form. It is obviously not a poem. It is not purely a narrative, but it has important elements of narration. In is not purely an exposition. It is not just argumentation, but it may have important elements of argumentation. It is not just fiction, but… it may have important elements of a detective story.[5]

As you investigate the case situation, like a detective, you will find yourself immersed in the organisation and then you will begin to glean insights into the often unwritten or unspoken aspects of its culture and practices. All these insights will help you to develop a clearer picture of the situation that is being described within the narrative structure of the case (i.e., the *story* contained within the case study). This active engagement with the case study is what triggers your learning and is what educational scholars often refer to as *experiential learning.*

1.2 THE REFLECTIVE PRACTITIONER

The Kolb Cycle is a commonly referenced model of experiential learning that was first developed in 1974, which takes the participant through a four-stage process of learning that can then be repeated many times. Figure 1.1 provides an adapted version of the Kolb Cycle to demonstrate the function of reflective practice when learning with case studies. The model begins with a *concrete experience*. In this context, your experience is the case study class. The second stage involves reflective observation, which you are encouraged to undertake on completion of the case class discussion. This might involve asking yourself a series of reflective questions to determine the purpose and key learning from the class experience. Third, you consider *abstract conceptualisation* or, put another way, to develop generalisations that allow you to draw conclusions from the learning experience. And finally, *active experimentation* enables you to test the implications of these concepts in new situations and/or to try out what you have learned (perhaps by working them out in a subsequent case class). In a programme that contains multiple case studies, this repeated pattern of case study learning allows you to complete many successive cycles of the Kolb model and to effectively develop a learning strategy enabling you to capture learning that you can take with you back into your real world once the case sessions have ended.

At the end of each case discussion, you might be asked to prepare a report or some additional notes based on your class discussions to further promote reflective practice.

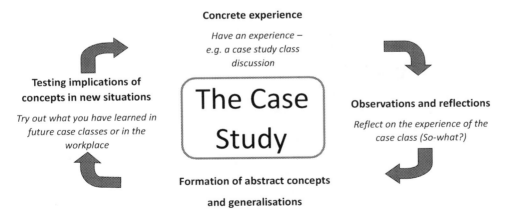

FIGURE 1.1 The Kolb Cycle Adapted for Case Studies

Regardless of what you are required to do next, the most important thing you need to do at the end of the session is to ask yourself...

1.3 SO WHAT?

In one of my very early undergraduate classes as a case tutor, I was horrified to overhear one of my top students leaving the classroom at the end of a case discussion, turning to her friend saying, "yeah, yeah, interesting case study, interesting story, so what?" At first, I was troubled that this student may not have grasped the key learning objectives of the session and so I started to think about how to mitigate against this. Over the years, however, I have become more and more inclined to positively encourage my students to ask themselves the 'so what?' question as a matter of good practice – indeed as the hallmark of an effective reflective practitioner.

The 'so what?' question enables you to detach yourself from the story itself and to consider what key learning 'takeaways' have been derived from this experience. This might include reflecting on what you know now that you didn't know before. Or what you understand differently to how you had seen things before.

If at the end of the session you

- know something you did not know before; or
- can do something (or do it better) than you could before; or
- have formed a view about something that you did not hold before

then you have learned. And the more you ask 'so what?', the more you 'takeaway' and the more you learn. This part of the case process is all about reflection. Some people are natural reflectors, I am not (although I wish I were), so I have to actively build reflection into my thinking to ensure that I don't miss out on the 'power of reflective practice'. We'll look at this more in Chapter 4. First of all, you need to consider how best to prepare for the case discussion and this is discussed in detail in the next chapter.

1.4 IN SUMMARY

In summary, this chapter has:

- introduced the concept of the case participant as a scholarly detective unearthing evidence to inform a discussion, an evaluation for analysis or conclusions about a particular situation;
- examined the four stages of reflective practice, commonly deployed in case method learning;
- identified the value of the case method as a well-established, global phenomenon, drawing from examples of scholars from different parts of the world.

NOTES

1 Ellet, 2018, p5.
2 Peter Killing, Professor of Strategy, quoted in Simmons, 2013.
3 Farhoomand, 2004, p103.
4 Cranston, 2008, p582.
5 McNair, 1971, p1.

CHAPTER 2

How Do I Prepare for a Case Discussion?

This chapter begins by examining the 'anatomy' of the case study, how each part of the case is developed and the purpose behind each part of the case. The chapter then goes on to explore seven points that you might wish to consider when preparing for a case. To help make sense of each 'consideration', a full case study is included to provide an illustration. At the end of this chapter, you should be aware of the key ingredients of an effective case experience, and the roles that you should adopt to achieve the best learning experience from a case session. You will also have the tools to deconstruct and analyse the case as part of your preparation for class discussion, working through several different approaches to your case preparation.

But first, let us see what other people from around the world have to say about how to prepare for a case discussion:

> Responsibility for analysis and conclusions about issues within the case rest with the students. The focus is on student learning through their own joint efforts. The case teacher's role is seen as one of guiding student discussion rather than providing answers.
>
> (The Case Centre, UK, 2015[1])

> To understand information, we have to have a way of organising it. Developing the skills to identify which... scenario... is at the core of a case solves one of the biggest problems of studying a case: how to meaningfully organise the information in it.
>
> (Harvard, US, 2018[2])

> Learning groups can act as an early warning system and faculty can reach out in the case of problems with the learning. For example, it can take a couple of months for students, especially those who are more shy and from certain backgrounds, to realise that the class discussion is risk free, but in time, with support, they all become used to it.
>
> (ESMT, Germany, 2019[3])

It is highly likely that your first exposure to the case method will be when your tutor hands you a case study and invites you to prepare it for a class discussion in a few days' time. But what does it mean to 'prepare it for discussion'? You may have been given a case tutorial beforehand to establish some ground rules or as part of your student induction

DOI: 10.4324/9781003345978-4

programme, or perhaps your first case class session might be something of an induction for you to develop understanding into how to work with and learn from cases. To help you get started, it is helpful to know something about the case study, how it is constructed and prepared by writers for use in class to help promote learning. Once armed with these details, you can then deconstruct your case as part of your initial analysis and preparation in advance of the class discussion. The case is a story about a management situation. Within that story there are likely to be issues that need to be addressed, perhaps decisions that need to be made, options that could be considered, data to be analysed and ultimately conclusions to be drawn.

The case could be sourced from primary or secondary data. The primary data will be sourced from either within the organisation or from contributors outside the organisation, looking in at the situation. The secondary data might be multi-sourced to eliminate any specific bias and ensure it provides a consistent, true-to-life perspective of what really happened in the organisation. Most often these are true stories, based on situations that have taken place in real organisations, although sometimes the names of the characters and the organisations may have been altered to provide anonymity or to protect confidentiality. Obviously where an organisation has been named then you are free to consider exploring other data accessible in the public domain on the same organisation to help you to build a clearer profile of the business and the likely events that led up to the situation(s) that are depicted in the case itself.

There are different types of case study and these 'types' are discussed in more detail in the next chapter but let us start by considering the way the case has been formatted for you. If it is a paper-based case, is it a single case narrative? Or might it be part of a series for which you have been given just the opening section? Are there questions that have been provided in addition to the case by your tutor, either separate to the case or as an integrated part of the case itself? These will provide some hints around the likely direction of the class discussion for which you are being asked to prepare the case. It is also worth considering the location of the case in the module that you are studying. For example, have you just completed a series where you have been exploring some specific type of management theory or model? If so, does the content of this subsequent case study lend itself to drawing insights from this previous theory or management model? Or put another way, could the scenario depicted within this case enable you to apply this new theory or model?

As you examine the case that has been presented to you there are four more things you might wish to consider: the issues, the data, their treatment and your analysis.

Are there many or few *issues* raised in the case? And are these issues related or independent of each other? Are all the issues likely to be relevant to the specific learning objectives of this class session (or the questions that may have been presented when the case was handed out)? It is possible that some cases may contain 'red herrings' or misleading data, as this is a justifiable reflection of the real world.

When looking at the *data* provided within the case, is there a lot or a little? If only a little, then arguably all the data that is present is likely to be valuable and will form a necessary part of your analysis. And second, is the data explicit or implicit within the text of the case? Sometimes data can be found in conveniently tabulated exhibits towards the end of the case study document and sometimes the data is sprawled across the whole of the core text of the case and your job will be to extract the relevant data (and where appropriate, tabulate it yourself), and discard what you consider to be the less relevant data.

The *treatment* of the case relates to the mode of thinking required to address the issues raised in the case. In some circumstances, the tutor may have issued the case to allow you to apply a theory or model recently discussed in class – this is sometimes referred to as deductive learning. In other scenarios, it may be that the case discussion is more exploratory, which leads to the development of a particular type of theory or approach – a treatment often referred to as an inductive approach. Sometimes the data will need to be captured, tabulated and then analysed to form a clearer picture of the situation – this is sometimes referred to as a convergent or analytical treatment of the data; while other approaches might be more free-flowing and creative in their construct, leading to a divergent and creative response from the class discussion.

Finally, when it comes to *analysing* your case data, is there only one likely answer that can be derived? Or might the case offer more than one particular type of response? Often cases tend to promote the latter, and if so then your job might be to consider how you would argue the adequacy of your preferred choice of response, by comparing the benefits and pitfalls of each option that presents itself. Remember, in management not all things are black and white. There may be some black and white (or to use a detective phrase: open and shut) cases, but often amid the black and white is a lot of 'grey' and it is this 'grey-space' that is subject to your interpretation.

2.1 SEVEN PRINCIPAL CONSIDERATIONS

There are seven general principles or questions that you might wish to consider as part of your case preparation. These are listed below as a starter and then each one is unpacked later in this chapter:

1.   What are the key issues of the case?
2.   Who are the key stakeholders?
3.   What extra data would it be helpful to access in order to more fully appraise the issues raised in the case? And where will I find this?
4.   What skills are being tested in this case?
5.   Are there any case snags or hidden issues?
6.   What management theory, models or learning tools could inform your case analysis or help you to make-sense of the issues?
7.   Are there any clues in the *case opening* and/or *case closure*?

To help make sense of each of these questions, have a look at the Black Sheep Brewery Case Study, which is a field-researched case study that explores the first five years of a new business venture: the launch of a brewery. This brewery went on to become a very successful international business. This particular story is based on conversations with the brewery's founder and raises some interesting points for discussions, both from a leadership and a marketing perspective.

2.2 CASE STUDY: BLACK SHEEP BREWERY[4]

It is hard to imagine that so much activity could thrive around such a tiny village in the heart of the Yorkshire Dales in Northern England. Masham had always been an important landmark for UK brewing and the establishment of Black Sheep Brewery in 1992 had encouraged this longstanding tradition to continue.

You only had to take a sip of the cool brown ale to slip away into a nostalgic haze between reality and the rural idyll. However, times change and the dynamics of the UK brewery industry bring you reeling back to your senses, as Paul Theakston, company director, knows only too well:

> The Big Boys are fighting for market share, and therefore the discounts out there in the trade are becoming quite outrageous. We can't even begin to play in that game, but, nonetheless, we are having to stay in touch with it. It's a relativity thing.

2.2.1 The History of the Business

The story of the Black Sheep brewery is a true depiction of a 'country' brewery, in contrast with the macro-brewers or what Theakston termed "the Burton and London biggies." The brewing of all their beers used very traditional vessels and ingredients, and was fermented exclusively in Yorkshire slate squares. Only proven techniques that had been established for many years were employed and consequently they produced only real ales of an excellent quality.

The brewery was set up by Paul Theakston as a Business Expansion Scheme in 1992. Shares were allocated for sale over a two-month period, up to a maximum of £750,000. This scheme offered shareholders tax-free benefits for a period of five years, as well as enabling the brewery to be fairly well capitalised from the beginning. In 1993, a second business expansion scheme raised a further £750,000. The brewery grew to accommodate 690 shareholders, providing sufficient investments to permit all activities to be funded through the brewery's own earnings.

Paul Theakston himself came from a very long line of brewers. The brand Theakston's, that was eventually acquired by Scottish Courage, was traditionally brewed in Masham by his father and uncle. Paul joined the family business at the Theakston Brewery, and only left there after Scottish and Newcastle (now Scottish Courage) took them over in 1987.

Black Sheep's annual turnover grew to more than £4.5 million and in 1996 they invested £300,000 into the construction of a fascinating visitor centre, incorporating a large shop, bistro and video area. Between the brewery and the visitor centre, Black Sheep employed 62 people and their weekly output from the brewery grew to as many as 500 barrels.

The brewery was too large to be categorised as a micro-brewery, yet not large enough to fit into the classification of a 'full blooded' regional. Sitting at the helm, and slowly emptying the glass of the brown ale, Paul continued:

> We don't really fit into a specific slot – we are having to portray that although we are growing, we are still a very small company in terms of the high standards of service that we can offer, i.e., we are not into this faceless monolith concept, however, we are big enough to offer the services that the bigger breweries provide, such as cellar services and the installation and maintenance of beer pumps, etc.

In the on-trade sector, their draught beer, which represented 70% of their total sales, was very much a regional brand of North Yorkshire, Newcastle, Huddersfield, M62 corridor etc., being sold to over 300 outlets within a 70-mile radius of Masham. Only one fifth of their draught beer production was sold to wholesalers: "We are self-limiting concerning our on-trade sales, as we only have the fermenting capacity for a maximum of 500 barrels per week."

In the off-trade sector of the market, Theakston stated: "We have pseudo-national coverage." Thirty per cent of their total beer sales was through the sale of bottled beer into the take-home sector. The main UK distributors of their products were Marks & Spencer, Sainsbury's, Tesco, Waitrose, Asda, Safeways and Morrisons.

Marks & Spencer had been distributing their 'Special' ale for four and a half years. The deal itself was not hugely profitable, however the kudos associated with supplying such a reputable name, had a very significant effect on the reputation of the brewery:

> This deal has stood us well, especially when trying to persuade other supermarkets to stock our beers. It has given us a seal of approval and a seal of quality.

Black Sheep beer was stocked in 150 Tesco outlets nationwide, located primarily in the bigger stores with greater shelf space and offering the widest variety of beers. Sainsbury's were by far the greatest distributor, with the majority of their stores stocking Black Sheep beers.

2.2.2 Marketing the Business

From an annual turnover of £4.5 million, Black Sheep spent approximately £65,000 on marketing the entire business. This was split between the main business and the visitor centre, the former representing £45,000 of this figure, and the latter £20,000.
The promotional split for 1996, was as follows:

Promotional tool	%
Advertising	75%
Public relations	5%
Sponsorship	5%
Point of sale material	75%
Direct selling	10%

2.2.2.1 Advertising

Black Sheep had been in the enviable position of receiving high-profile, free advertising and publicity through no conscious effort of their own. The business did not entertain any television or radio advertising, preferring to focus on press coverage. Occasionally this took the form of an advertisement in *The Star* newspaper, but the majority of their press advertising in newspapers and local periodicals was aimed at supporting specific events or activities, for example, supporting a particular promotional event in a pub, etc. Theakston commented: "We don't tend to do 'generic' advertising." He then continued to explain the predominant reason for their low advertising spend:

> I don't mean to sound arrogant, but we have always been faced with a very nice problem. Selling our beer has not caused us any difficulties because we have always been able to sell as much as we have wanted to – our problem, has been matching capacity with demand. Due to this, we have not really been pushed into a lot of advertising; we haven't needed to bump up our sales and so therefore have avoided a lot of expense.

It was, however, the unintentional advertising coverage that Black Sheep received over its lifetime, which had the most far-reaching effects on its success. The brewery's huge publicity was attributed to two major factors. First, Paul Theakston himself, was a very respected and recognised name within the brewery industry. Second, Theakston set up the Black Sheep brewery a stone's throw away from the old Theakston Brewery which was taken over by Scottish and Newcastle in 1987. "The huge publicity that we received was all to do with the 'David and Goliath' situation – we were setting up business next door to 'Big Brother'." He continued:

> In the beginning, we were bombarded by every newspaper in the book as well as numerous television channels – it was all free! Although we cannot take the credit for the free publicity, we certainly did use it to the very best of our advantage.

It was this publicity that was so very powerful in advertising the company when it was first established. "It lifted the profile of our very young company, very quickly, and without us having to spend a penny of our own money."

2.2.2.2 Public Relations

Although the purpose of the Visitor's Centre had always been first and foremost to generate profit, it was also certainly the brewery's most efficacious PR tool. The centre had been designed to the highest of standards to provide an atmosphere most conducive for visitors to come and browse. Everything that the shop sold had a black sheep somewhere on it, constantly reinforcing the brewery image in the minds of the public. The restaurant served very high-quality, freshly cooked food, and people would often visit the centre solely for a meal and a drink, which again helped to raise the profile of the brewery.

Tours were conducted around the brewery on a very regular basis, all year round, terminating in the visitor centre with a meal and a pint of Black Sheep ale. Throughout the run up to Christmas, the visitor centre was also a very popular venue for company Christmas parties.

One company shareholder, an executive producer of the popular TV programme *Emmerdale*, decided that it would be an ideal PR stunt to show Black Sheep on the set, in the Woolpack – the TV serial's fictional public house. Black Sheep bar towels, beer mats, pump clips and bottles became all part of the *Emmerdale* 'stage furniture'.

Finally, the brewery made a concerted effort to support local craftsmen and other businesses, by stocking local, hand-crafted items in the gift shop.

2.2.2.3 Sponsorship

Sponsorship had been encouraged to build positive relationships with the local community, while raising general public awareness for the brewery. Unlike most other breweries sporting events were avoided in favour of sponsoring the 'arts'. A more recent campaign had involved the funding of a local theatre group, who were performing a play called *Mac the Sheep Stealer*. As Theakston explained:

> This seemed a more than appropriate play for us to sponsor. It not only gives us the opportunity to offer support to the local community, but it also helps to reinforce our image.

2.2.2.4 Point of Sale Material

The brewery had placed a high priority on this promotional tool, and the materials used were to the highest standard. Beer mats, bar towels, pump clips, to name but a few, had been distributed around public houses that serve their beers, to complement T-shirts for all bar staff which came with the logo 'Baa Staff'.

All of the promotional themes and ideas were generated in-house – Theakston being very sceptical about marketing agencies, referring to them as "a complete waste of money."

2.2.2.5 *Direct Selling*

Before the brewery was opened in 1992, Black Sheep had employed a salesman in the previous summer, who spent a large amount of time out in the trade, looking for potential outlets in which to sell their beer. By the time production began in the following April, 75 public houses had agreed to trial it – 55 of those were still loyal customers five years later. Cold selling was then conducted for the next two years. Within five years the demand for their beer became greater than their brewing capacity, and as such, the need for direct selling diminished.

2.2.3 The Success of the Company

Black Sheep has been an archetypal representation of a 'success story'. Theakston attributes their achievements to several underlying factors. First, he remarked:

> I personally started with an advantage from the beginning, due to my background. Over the last five years, Theakston's has become a truly national brand which has certainly helped to establish my name.

Second, Theakston explained that having been in the industry for such a long time, it was easier for him to avoid the common pitfalls, which people get entrapped in so often. The two most common snares that people within the industry fall prey to are regarding quality and the speed at which the business grows:

> Sustaining beer quality is of prime importance. Many of the smaller breweries make the tragic mistake of "finding out how to do it" whilst they are trading. Unfortunately, it only takes one or two "duff" batches, before you really damage your reputation, especially during the "tender flower stage".

Black Sheep had an excellent record of maintaining consistency in their quality, and as a result, they soon developed a very good reputation for quality.

Regarding the speed of growth, Theakston explained:

> We are not growing too quickly on purpose. When I was at Theakston's, there were three or four years, where we grew exponentially, literally doubling our sales every year. It puts such a huge strain on everything – personnel, finances, quality standards etc.

Theakston noted that they had no urge for the brewery to grow too big, as they had no intentions of brewing off-site:

We see ourselves as a single site brewery, and we intend to continue brewing Black Sheep only here in Masham. Theakston's is sold by Scottish and Newcastle, as a product of tradition and heritage, having its roots firmly based in Masham, however, when they are producing 4500 barrels of it per week they are obviously not brewing it all in Masham by any means. If Black Sheep were not brewed in Masham, then it would not be the genuine article.

2.2.4 The Challenges for Tomorrow's Market

In conclusion, Theakston was the first to admit how successful the brewery had been during its first five years. However, he illustrated that the harsh marketing environment had affected them over this period:

> The outlook we had when we began, and the reality we have experienced regarding our profits over the last five years, have been greatly different. The greatest variance, has been regarding the "bottom line" – it has not grown as fast as we initially anticipated, and this is all attributable to ever-increasingly squeezed margins.

Pondering these thoughts for a few moments one began to wonder what were the real opportunities and threats that lay ahead for the company. A forthcoming meeting of the shareholders would be sure to provide the opportunity for some challenging questions and Theakston's vision for the future would play a critical role in encouraging ongoing shareholder investment.

2.3 ANALYSING THE CASE STUDY

Now that you have read the case study, let us look at the steps you could go through to prepare this case for a class discussion, using the list of seven principal considerations from earlier in this chapter. But before that, can I invite you to go through the case study again and this time read it slower and in more detail. You may even wish to highlight certain parts of the case study (provided this is your own copy of the book!). When I read through a case, I tend to read it three times. First, I have a quick read to take in the whole narrative structure of the case (i.e., to read and enjoy the story). My second read is the deep-dive where I make notes, and my third read is to cross reference this to the case questions to make sure there is nothing else I have missed out. In my second read-through I note three things. First, I tend to underline or highlight every time that 'time' is mentioned. This helps me to get a feel for the chronology or time-structure of the case. Most cases are not written with a linear chronological structure so sometimes it can be helpful to avoid confusion by extracting this information to develop your own timeline of events. Second, I will use a separate colour to highlight the names of every stakeholder in the case study (so I can get a feel for all the different perspectives that I might wish to consider later in my analysis). And third, if I have a question forming in my head as I read a particular part of the case, then I will note this, in the relevant margin in the text, to come back to later. Having done this, I am now ready to reflect on my seven principal considerations:

Principal consideration 1: What are the key issues of the case?
This case has been described as a 'David and Goliath' story, as further industry research would identify that the Black Sheep Brewery emerged as a new brewery during a period where many other breweries were either going out of business or being merged and acquired by larger breweries. What's more, this new brewery was built immediately adjacent to a macro brewery, Theakston Brewery, and the founder of this new Black Sheep Brewery was himself a member of the infamous Theakston family of brewers. Paul Theakston had capitalised on this story as he – the black sheep – built the reputation of this new, small brewery on the status of his family name. His leadership and decision-making in this difficult time of new business development would be key to the organisation's survival or failure.

This new business venture was capitalised by 690 shareholders through a Business Expansion Scheme that offered shareholders tax-free benefits for a period of five years. Having shunned more conventional promotional methods, Paul relied on industry contacts, carefully choreographed media attention and his personal reputation to raise awareness and the profile of the business. The emergence of this new business with its 'David and Goliath' dimension had attracted huge media publicity, with little need for marketing investment. But is this a sustainable business development model? What type of leadership style is needed to ensure future business survival? And how will marketing planning ensure the organisation is best positioned to thrive in the future?

Principal consideration 2: Who are the key stakeholders?
It is always helpful to consider a full list of the stakeholders in any case as this allows you to potentially consider the challenges raised in the case by reflecting from different viewpoints and perspectives. Clearly the most obvious stakeholder in the story of Black Sheep Brewery is Paul Theakston, a master brewer from a long line of family brewers, based in Masham, North Yorkshire; but he is not the only stakeholder that should be considered in this story. Black Sheep employed 62 people and the business was initially capitalised by 690 shareholders through a Business Expansion Scheme. Paul Theakston is only one member of the Theakston family and other family members may have lesser stakeholder roles to consider too. And finally, don't forget 'Goliath': Theakston Brewery is only a few metres away in the same small village. How might this 'giant' respond to Black Sheep Brewery's growth plans?

Principal consideration 3: What extra data would it be helpful to access in order to more fully appraise the issues raised in the case? And where will I find this?
This is based on a real organisation, so a little time spent internet searching will provide a lot of material on the organisation that will help to provide a context for this case study. The main thing to watch out for when checking websites is that they may not reflect the actual activities facing the organisation at the point at which the case was written. For example, the company may have changed its branding priorities, invested differently in marketing and changed its leadership since the case was first written, all of which might serve to paint a different picture to that which is captured in the case itself. The company will have to publish its annual reports and these are publicly accessible with further internet searching. Historical reports should also be available, which will enable you

to consider trends for the organisation over time. As this case study is located in the heart of the UK brewery industry, it may help to look a little wider at the sector as a whole – its mergers and acquisitions and the way in which the sector is structured. For example, a brief search of the sector's online sites will enable you to quickly identify that there are several different segments to the UK brewery sector from mainstream, mass-produced beers, to speciality beers, to regional beers and international ales.

Principal consideration 4: What skills are being tested in this case?
Case studies invite audience participation, or in other words, you are invited to get involved in the case and share your own perspectives. This is normally facilitated by your case instructor and there may be a number of different skills that your tutor might be looking for you to develop as you are invited to prepare for the case discussion. Sometimes, the questions provided along with the case in advance of the discussion hold some clues towards the types of skills which might be called upon. These could include:

- Analysis and critical thinking
- Decision-making
- Judging between courses of action
- Handling assumptions and inferences
- Presenting different points of view
- Listening to and understanding others
- Relating theory to practice

From the limited data contained within this case two things are reasonably clear: first, that the founder pays little regard to spending money on marketing and, so far, has chosen to draw on his own reputation and standing within the community to capitalise on free publicity. But this is finite and may therefore need a rethink to support the ongoing development of the company after its initial 'honeymoon' period. As such, you may be called upon to propose your own marketing plan for the company and argue the adequacy of your preferred choices. Second, there is an indication at the very end of the case that an impending shareholder meeting is due. This lends itself to a role-play scenario between Paul, his management team and the shareholders. This again, may require you to deploy certain communication skills as you prepare to potentially play one of these roles. It also, therefore, invites you to consider the challenges facing the organisation from different viewpoints.

Principal consideration 5: Are there any case snags or hidden issues?
Often there are hidden challenges contained 'between the lines' of the case study and these might require further unearthing before you can fully expose all the issues that need to be analysed in preparation for class discussion. These snags might include specialist terms that are used in the narrative structure and that might be unfamiliar to you as the reader. These may need further examining for clarification before proceeding further. The *narrative* structure is one of the four key structures of the case study, the others being the *chronology* (time) structure, the *expository* structure (the degree to which data is provided or hidden within the text) and the *plot* structure (the clash of individuals, ideas

and motivations). Case snags can often be found by closer examination of the *chronology* (time) structure. A timeline of the case study may unearth some interesting observations. The opening section of the Black Sheep Brewery case identifies that the organisation was capitalised by shareholders who were offered tax-free benefits for a period of five years as part of a government-led initiative to try to encourage investment in new business growth. All good things come to an end, and it is reasonable to assume that shareholders would have been most likely to reconsider their investment as the five-year tax-free period comes to a close. Fast forward to the end of the case, and we read of the founder, Paul, preparing for his organisation's quinquennial meeting of the shareholders – five years after the business had been set-up. This sheds a new perspective on the meeting as it is likely that shareholders would have needed to be convinced of why they should continue to invest in the company once the tax-free incentives had ceased. Without an appraisal of the timeline for this case study, it would have been easy to miss this key hidden issue.

Principal consideration 6: What management theory, models or learning tools could inform your case analysis or help you to make sense of the issues?
The questions that accompany a case may provide a clue of the types of theories, models or tools that can be employed to best support your appraisal of the case data. In the case of Black Sheep Brewery, it is likely that such models might relate either to leadership practices or to marketing planning and strategies. As this case also refers repeatedly to the *performance* of the organisation the adoption of a *SWOT analysis* might provide a useful starting point for an appraisal of the organisation's performance.

Principal consideration 7: Are there any clues in the case opening and/or case closure?
Case writers often adopt a practice of making important keynote statements about the issues raised in the case in the opening and closing paragraphs of the text. One Harvard professor discussing a typical approach to case writing stated that in the opening paragraph of the case, the case writer would normally make a statement about the issue which must be decided in the company. In the second paragraph the writer would give a little background about the company and its place in the industry, and in the third paragraph tell how the situation requiring action developed. After which, additional data should be provided about how the management handled earlier events leading up to the issue, including data from which alternative courses of action might be visualised.

The challenge for the case writer is to *keep the main thing the plain thing* and this is often achieved by ensuring that the main issue is captured in the opening section of the case and then reinforced in the closing section of the case. This does not always happen, but it is worth checking to see if clear themes are present in both. The Black Sheep Brewery case begins by including a quote from Paul stating that there is a lot of pressure to safeguard market-share. The quote included provocative statements such as: "the big boys are fighting" and "We can't even begin to play in that game." These statements give an indication of the tensions facing this new brewery. Even though Paul seems to have ridden the wave of media popularity for five years, the case's closing sections include statements such as: "Unfortunately, it only takes one or two 'duff' batches, before you really damage your reputation, especially during the 'tender flower stage'" and "regarding the 'bottom line' – it has not grown as fast as we initially anticipated, and this is all attributable to ever-increasingly squeezed margins." This provides a clear indication that tensions continue to exist for Paul as he prepares for this quinquennial shareholder meeting – tensions that will no doubt be the subject of questions from wavering shareholders.

2.4 FURTHER SUPPORT FOR CASE PREPARATION

There are a number of other resources available to help you to prepare for your case class discussion. In recent years, The Case Centre and Harvard Business Publishing have produced really helpful resources to assist students in case class preparation. The Case Centre has produced an interactive study guide for students to help guide you through the case preparation process. This interactive guide (which can be found at www.thecasecentre.org/guide) incorporates videos, quizzes, templates and an embedded case study with worked-out examples to help you navigate through four distinct stages of case preparation. There is a *case analysis template* included within this online resource which you can use to work through a full case study example that is embedded in the study guide, after which you can download it and use it as a future template to work on your own in-class case studies.

Harvard has more recently produced its own study guide as an interactive introduction to case study analysis. More details of this can be found in Chapter 15.

2.5 IN SUMMARY

In summary, this chapter has:

- introduced you to certain aspects of the anatomy of a case study;
- provided a list of questions that you should consider when preparing a case for class discussion;
- included a full case study with a worked-out application of these questions;
- signposted you to other resources that you can access to provide further support for case preparation.

NOTES

1 Heath, 2015, p9.
2 Ellet, 2018, p17.
3 Zoltán Antal-Mokos quoted in Simmons, 2019, p2.
4 This case was developed by the author and was derived from published materials and personal experience, incorporating student research conducted for Scott Andrews, now published at the Royal Agricultural University, Cirencester, UK.

CHAPTER 3

What Types of Case Study Are Used in Classes?

There are principally eight different types of case study, each of which are examined in closer detail in this chapter. You may find yourself reviewing different cases in different ways according to their structure and design, their learning objectives, and the specific subject themes that are being covered in your course. An understanding of the different types of case will enable you to adapt your preparation for class discussion. Some types of case can be found in greater frequency in certain specific areas of subject matter, so it is worth considering this as you look at how different cases are structured and formatted in different subject modules on your programme. For example, it is unlikely that a case used in a Finance and Accounting module will be structured in the same way as a case study prepared for a Leadership and Change Management module. Before an author submits a case to The Case Centre, case writers are required to determine what type of case they are writing by subject matter as part of their case submission process, and these are the categories of subject matter that case writers normally have to choose between:

- Economics, Politics and Business Environment
- Entrepreneurship
- Ethics and Social Responsibility
- Finance, Accounting and Control
- Human Resource Management/Organisational Behaviour
- Knowledge, Information and Communications Systems Management
- Marketing
- Production and Operations Management
- Strategy and General Management

Interestingly, The Case Centre has introduced a more recent requirement for case writers to consider which of the United Nations Sustainable Development Goals (SDG) are also addressed by the case study, which demonstrates a growing global awareness for cases to reflect these important SDG themes.

The next sections of this chapter compare each of the eight most commonly considered types of case study, by design and content.

DOI: 10.4324/9781003345978-5

3.1 SITUATION CASE

> The student is asked to make an analysis of the information embodied in the case and to delineate the significant relationships existing among the various items of data. This often involves the question "why did things go wrong and how could this have been avoided?"
>
> (The Case Centre, UK, 2015[1])

One of the most traditional and popular forms of case has been the situation case, which tends to include a description of a situation or a sequence of events and activities for which there is likely to be more than one probable set of responses and subsequent outcomes. These situation case studies remain the most popular type of case in management education, and are frequently found in Strategy, Marketing, Human Resource and Operations Management programmes.

This classic case approach often invites you to step into the shoes of the key protagonist within the story and to consider the various options available as the situation unfolds.

One example of a situation case is 'Leadership for Sustainable Healthcare', which is listed as a case study derived from published sources and which clearly reflects some level of general experience. It was written by Stefi Barna, Emma Thompson and Aditya Vyas of Medact (United Kingdom) and was produced as part of an Erasmus+ funded programme involving Medical Peace Work (www.medicalpeacework.org). You will find a copy of the full version of this case towards the end of this chapter in section 3.10, and the case is also available as a free case at www.thecasecentre.org. You will note from the layout of the text that, as this case is derived from published sources, there are weblinks that the authors have used to support your journey through the case without distracting from the general narrative (storytelling) structure, and these are listed in a table in the middle of the case. While listed by the authors as a Specialist Management case study, the situation described within the case covers a range of different topics including healthcare management, sustainability, sustainable healthcare, climate change, carbon reduction, triple bottom line, health leadership, service improvement, nursing, medicine, nephrology, general practice, and psychiatry.

The authors consider that the case could be used in two ways. This case has been written in a manner that allows it to be used both for specialist clinical healthcare-related subjects and for general leadership and management practice. Clearly the themes of sustainability and sustainable healthcare management are highly attractive in today's context. It is worth noting that the global health system is a significant contributor to greenhouse gas emissions, waste and pollution and as such, healthcare is among the most energy-intensive – and therefore carbon-intensive – business sectors. In Europe, evidence suggests that the carbon footprint of the healthcare sector accounts for at least 5% of the EU's carbon emissions.

The situation follows the case of a junior hospital nurse who investigates the possibilities for increased healthcare efficiencies that will result in reduced costs, better patient care and less waste. The case ends with a number of questions that could be used to inform the direction of a classroom discussion. If you wanted to explore the case study, and have little or no clinical experience, then it is proposed that you could review Mr Williams' story from the case and for each encounter he has with the health system, to identify the areas where waste could have been reduced and patient care improved.

3.2 COMPLEX CASE

I've occasionally heard the case study compared to a jigsaw puzzle. When you are given the case, it is as if you are handed a box of jigsaw pieces and your job is to start putting the pieces together to form the image that displays the situation that is requiring analysis and review. Now imagine if you were handed a box with lots of extra peripheral pieces and even some pieces that didn't necessarily relate to the picture at all. Now you have a *complex case*.

These complex cases were traditionally produced as very large paper-based case studies, frequently used particularly in postgraduate study or for executive programmes. In complex cases, the case content incorporates data highly relevant to the case situation intermixed with less significant data, or even some data that may be irrelevant. The principal purpose behind this form of case is to challenge you to make judgements regarding the quality of the data and to extract the relevant data from the less relevant data before then considering a response to the challenges set by the case objectives. It is quite common for students to challenge the usefulness of these types of lengthy paper-based cases today, which is justifiable to a certain degree, but don't forget the internet presents similar challenges for businesses today, when analysts need to search for relevant evidence from the vast quantities of less relevant data available online. Sometimes today's case writers generate complex cases by creating a case narrative that signposts you to online resources from which you can then exercise your own judgement to determine the relevant data from less relevant online data. The complex nature and purpose of the case study remains the same, but the context is shifted from the paper to the screen.

3.3 DECISION-MAKING CASE

As a detective, my Dad would often find himself in court cases where decisions needed to be taken based on the evidence that had been revealed from the investigations. In a similar way, case studies that provide descriptions of situations will often lead you to a point where the protagonist from the case is required to make a decision. The classic *decision-making* case study would normally provide at least two or three likely and feasible approaches to a certain issue facing the organisation. Your challenge is to exercise judgement to determine the most appropriate option, while considering the merits and pitfalls of each of the other options, and hence to present a balanced argument when considering how an organisation should respond to the decisions raised within the case.

> Of the cases you read, the most frequent type of scenario will probably be a decision. That reflects the real world in which organizations constantly make decisions. In a business course that uses cases, you're therefore very likely to have to write about decision scenario cases.
>
> (Harvard, US[2])

One example of a decision case is the 'Seat Belts in School Buses Controversy', which is listed as a field research case study. It was written by Professor John Phillimore and Alan Tapper from Curtin University in Australia and was produced as part of the Case Program of the Australia and New Zealand School of Government (ANZSOG). You will find a copy of the full version of this case towards the end of this chapter in section 3.10, and the case is also available as a free case at www.thecasecentre.org. You will note from the layout of the case that there are references that the authors have used to support the case's development, and these are also listed at the end of the case. While listed by the authors as a Strategy and General Management case study, the situation described within the case covers a range of different topics including cost–benefit analysis, delivery of services, health and safety, implementation/evaluation, infrastructure, transport, utilities, issues management, ministerial relationships, political environment, moral panic, public transport, road safety, road transport, and strategic communication.

The authors consider that the case could be viewed in two parts, the first being the political story up to the decision by the Australian government of whether to make seat belts compulsory, and the second being its implementation process. The case study explores a number of points including:

- The key decisions during the policy-making process.
- The role of each of the relevant stakeholders in influencing policy.
- The role of evidence in public debate and public service advice.
- The challenges for public sector managers and their political leaders in judging 'public value'.

As you read through the case, here are two questions you might consider:

- Should the government bow to public and media pressure to decide to make seat belts compulsory?
- Assuming that seat belts do become compulsory, how should the implementation process be handled?

3.4 QUANTITATIVE (EXERCISE) CASE

Many types of decision cases involve people, opinions, and data. Those with larger data sets tend to require far more in-depth analysis and number crunching. These *quantitative cases* are often referred to as exercise cases and tend to prove very effective in subject areas, such as accounting, finance, business planning and big data analytics. They normally require you to undertake some form of exercise (treatment) with the data to determine a set of outcomes. For example, this might be drawing data from the narrative to form a *profit and loss* statement or a *balance sheet* for an organisation. These types of exercises might provide a single 'right or wrong' answer, but this isn't normally the end goal of the case. Having completed the *number-crunching* exercises, the next step is to exercise judgement to determine what these details tell you about the organisation in the context of the situation it is facing.

In some examples *exercise cases* will contain lots of data provided in an ad hoc fashion throughout the case text, and in other examples an exercise case might contain all of its numerical data in nicely ordered and tabulated exhibits included at the end of the case narrative. In both examples, your challenge is to identify and extract the relevant data and consider how it should be reordered in order to undertake the necessary analysis to achieve the objectives (or questions) of the case.

> Push the numbers, play with the numbers and you may get a much better feel for the whole situation…. One has to be careful however not to get lost in detailed numerical analysis with little reflection about what these numbers actually mean.
>
> (Richard Ivey School of Business, Canada[3])

3.5 BACKGROUND CASE

By contrast, a more descriptive case can lack both plot, people, and the need for decision-making. These types of cases, often referred to as *background cases*, tend to be more popular as scene-setters, when looking to develop a broader understanding around a particular theme. For example, the tutor may wish to run a module that explores a number of strategic decisions made by different motor manufacturers, and so they may have selected appropriate cases from a range of different companies. The background case can serve as a popular prerequisite with which to explore an overview of the motor industry – its trends, themes, mergers and acquisitions over time. These exploratory background cases enable all the class participants to come to a certain point of knowledge and awareness, through macro environmental and economic analysis, from which to then begin exploring individual organisational cases.

3.6 INCIDENT CASE

The *incident case* is a highly popular short, often single-issue, case that the tutor can bring into a lecture or class discussion. These types of cases tend to require no pre-planning on the part of the students and can often serve as a useful breakout exercise, to change the pace of study in what might otherwise be a lengthy lecture session. They tend to allow the learner to apply a single concept or approach in a specific context, and can be useful tools for discovery, application and reflection.

> Although used less widely than the most conventional situation case, short case incidents can be a useful teaching vehicle. They can be introduced into a class to illustrate a lecture point or provide the basis for an exercise. One attraction of the incident is its brevity, it can be issued at any time and read in a few seconds.
>
> (The Case Centre, UK[4])

Sometimes these cases are referred to as *caselets* or *compact* cases, and they tend to be little more than one or two pages in length. They are useful cases for tutors to draw from when working with students who are less familiar or confident with the case method, as they normally require little preparation and tend not to be over-complex, as one *compact case* tutor explains:

> Compact Cases are a specialized form of teaching case study. Typically used in business schools, a Compact Case is a teaching case of fewer than 1000 words in length. Designed to be read in 15 minutes or less.
>
> (Westfield State University, US[5])

One example of an incident case is 'James Walker and the Line Manager', which is a short incident case study based on general experience. You will find a copy of the full version of this case towards the end of this chapter in section 3.10. As you read this case you will instantly be aware that this is a much shorter case than others provided in this book and can be read and assimilated in a few minutes. While the case does not include any specific dates, there is an obvious chronology structure, so it is relatively straightforward to plot the timeline for this narrative. There are four different perspectives that could be considered: Bryan, James, the other team members and their clients. The situation described within this short case explores a line management dilemma between a relatively new recruit (who has been on the team for 18 months) and his line manager. The case could be used for a HRM, Coaching and Mentoring, Leadership or Organisational Behaviour programme.

Despite its brevity the case study explores a number of points including:

- Managing competing challenges between teamworking and the development of strong consultant-client relationships.
- The likely impact of working with colleagues from different cultural backgrounds.
- The role of each of the stakeholders in managing the performance of the company.

As you read through the case, here are three questions you might consider:

- What are the challenges facing Bryan as he prepares for a conversation with James?
- How might James' current work practices have been informed by his former work experiences prior to joining St Stephens Solutions?
- What other reasons might James' colleagues have for raising concerns about his performance and how might Bryan investigate these prior to speaking with James?

3.7 DARKSIDE CASES

More recently there has been a growing body of case researchers contributing to what has become known as the *dark side of business*. The rationale for these cases is based on the following premise:

> Case libraries are almost exclusively devoted to "best practice" cases or difficult decisions by basically well-managed firms. When we want to talk to our students about the more typical cases, let alone the really scandalous practices of the worst firms, the cupboard is almost entirely bare. It's almost impossible to even find a reasonably rich case on a labor/management conflict.[6]

The *dark side case series* emerged from the Critical Management Studies Interest Group (CMSIG) at the Academy of Management and has grown to become a regular annual competition. As the name implies, this is a great place to go to when exploring some of the more complex, ethical and often scandalous elements of business and management. The Dark Side Case Competition was established to build interest and participation in case writing, to develop new cases for teaching based on a broad range of themes including the integration of socio-political issues with organisational dynamics, with a specific focus on organisational and management problems within capitalist systems. Many of these cases draw insights from business ethics and explore the notion that so-called 'ideal-type' cases also need to recognise the wider social, political and economic factors that shape managerial decisions. While originating in the US, this network has grown to attract cases from across the world including New Zealand, Canada, France and South Africa. Further details about this can be found in the final section of this book. For example, the Dark Side Case Competition winners in 2022 were derived from authors based at Wilfrid Laurier University and from Lazaridis School of Business & Economics, both located in Canada (and the winners from 2021 were located in business schools in Brazil).

3.8 LIVE CASES

Finally, the live case is a very different type of case to those previously described and presents a very vivid and real challenge to students, often through introducing real people who bring their own organisational issues to the class:

We find that the live case approach is an effective form of Work Integrated Learning, offering large numbers of students an authentic learning experience. We recommend this approach to universities seeking to offer large cohorts of students a workplace learning experience that is less time and resource dependent than internships.

(Tasmanian School of Business and Economics, Australia[7])

Experiential projects such as this make for richer teaching experiences for the faculty as well as receiving positive feedback from a majority of the students. In addition, [live cases enabled] the opportunity to observe students handling difficult tasks involving both project management and communication skills.

(Western New England College, US[8])

These types of cases are highly popular for Leadership, Change Management and Consultancy class groups. The success of these fast-emerging approaches to the case method have been evidenced across the world from the US to New Zealand, and more recently there has been a growth in this type of case development at business schools based in Turkey. At the heart of the live case is a business leader coming to class to present a real and current business problem, inviting you and your student peers to help find a solution or recommendation to the challenges outlined by the visit. Research has demonstrated that across cultures this type of case study provides a genuine, engaging and realistic insight as they enable you to capture a vivid real picture, in contrast to a hypothetical or distant business situation from a paper-based case. If you find your classes have become over-reliant on paper cases based on remote or distant companies that are unlikely to be the type of organisation you might find yourself working in at some point in the future, or facing problems that are alien to you and not really of direct perceivable value, then it is easy for you to start feeling disengaged by the lack of genuine applicability. By contrast, a live case fixes the context for the case on a situation that outplays itself right in front of your eyes, and which can therefore be shaped around localised agendas, cultures, traditions and approaches. While all previous forms of case content are rooted in the past, live cases are often presented in the current or even future tense. Live cases are discussed further in Chapter 7.

3.9 OTHER WAYS OF SEGMENTING TYPES OF CASE STUDIES

In addition to the typologies listed above, cases can be segmented according to their source of data or by their mode of presentation. Traditionally the case study was created by field researchers who had ventured into the organisation to gain first-hand experiences of the problems faced within the business. These days that can be an overcomplicated or costly process, so the emergence of more desk-based cases has led to bestselling cases based on secondary (or previously published) research outnumbering field data cases. The main point here for you to note is that if you look at the bottom of the first page of most case studies, you will most likely see a footnote that informs you whether this is based on field research or desk research. If it is exclusively derived from desk-based (previously published) research, then you can be sure that there is more data out there for you to go and explore should you feel you need to venture beyond the data contained within the actual case. Often these types of cases include bibliographies of the references used to research and develop the case and these can be valuable resources for your future research.

The benefits of *field research* cases are that they undoubtedly introduce new themes and fresh insights into real organisations including explorations of how a company's culture impacts on management functions. By contrast, *desk-based* cases based on previously published resources tend to provide broader perspectives on organisations as they tend to be multi-sourced to avoid any editorial biases. As the name implies, *general experience* cases tend to be developed by case writers who have been personally involved in some way within the organisation to which they are writing. As they reflect on their own general experiences, they can provide a single, deep dive into a particular organisational context but it is worth bearing in mind that they may be only presenting one perspective (their own) into the organisation rather than drawing broader insights from multiple stakeholders from within the organisation.

Another way of segmenting types of cases is by the way in which they are presented to you. As has already been stated, the traditional approach to the case method was to provide a large, paper-based story of a management situation in a single narrative style. More recently, there has been a growth in *sequential cases* or *case series*, which provide the same type of story but through the provision of numerous smaller bite-sized chunks of data. The giveaway here is when the case study title is post-texted with the figure 'A'. In this way, you might find yourself invited to read and prepare a case: '*Smith and Jones Ltd. A*' for class discussion. This shorter-than-usual case study will then be utilised by your class for discussion after which the tutor will then provide you with *Smith and Jones Ltd. B* to prepare for a future discussion. After this, *Smith and Jones Ltd. C, D* and *E* cases may follow which, when put together, provide the unfolding of a larger story with a broad and deep collection of data sets from which to help you derive insights into management practice. Figure 3.1 provides a summary of the typical approach to delivering a sequential case.

Given our preference for digital rather than paper-based study these days, it is perhaps not surprising that there is a growing number of video or multi-media type case studies available for case class discussion. Typical digital cases might include a single video case,

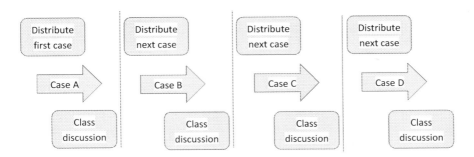

FIGURE 3.1 The Delivery Schedule for a Sequential Case

a more complex multi-media case or a simulation game. The peril with *video* cases is that you can easily switch off and become more passive in your association with the case material, so when you are watching a video case it will be very important to adopt the same approach to case preparation that was discussed in the previous chapter. Ensure you are taking notes and capturing key points as you review the video material (at least three times as part of your preparation). The more complex *multi-media case* can be developed into a multi-layered selection of case data, sometimes compared to either a *buffet meal* or *department shopping store*. The *buffet* analogy invites you to 'dip in' to take from different elements of the multi-layered case data as you make repeated 'visits to the table'. The *department store* analogy refers to the structuring of multi-media cases that can be analogous to different 'departments' of data, 'displayed' in different ways on different 'floors'. Your challenge is to ensure you have successfully navigated yourself through the whole 'store' and to be careful not to miss any crucial element of case data displayed in any of the departments, which would be needed to inform your overall case analysis. The *simulation game* is the closest the case study comes to the gamification of learning and will invite you to make real-time decisions about a particular situation from which the consequences of your choices enable you to customise your journey through the case data towards your personally determined conclusion. Learning from these types of multi-media cases will be explored in greater detail in Chapter 6.

3.10 EXAMPLES OF CASE STUDIES

This section includes three full cases, which provide illustrations of different types of case.

The first case is called 'Leadership for Sustainable Healthcare', which is an example of a typical *situation* case study. It was written by Stefi Barna, Emma Thompson and Aditya Vyas of Medact (United Kingdom), was produced as part of an Erasmus+ funded programme involving Medical Peace Work (www.medicalpeacework.org) and is reproduced with permission. The full case is also available as a free case at www.thecasecentre.org. Questions related to the case study can be found in section 3.1 of this chapter.

The second case is called 'The Seat Belts in School Buses Controversy', which is an example of a typical *decision* type case study. It was written by Professor John Phillimore and Alan Tapper from Curtin University in Australia and was produced as part of the Case Program of the Australia and New Zealand School of Government (ANZSOG) and is reproduced with permission. The full case is also available as a free case at www.thecasecentre.org. Questions related to the case study can be found in section 3.3 of this chapter.

The third case is called 'James Walker and the Line Manager' and is an example of a short *incident* case. Questions related to the case can be found in section 3.6 of this chapter.

3.10.1 Case Study: Leadership for Sustainable Healthcare[9]

3.10.1.1 Breaking Bad News

There was a sense of collective fatigue in the staff room of the Diabetes Centre and the early morning birdsong was punctuated by the clink of spoons in coffee cups. Sam sat down in one of the worn brown chairs by the window and picked up a newspaper. He was the newest addition to the nursing staff and eager to start the day. "Hey, have you seen this?" he grinned. "According to this article, obesity-related conditions will bankrupt the National Health Service by 2050!" He handed the newspaper to the nursing sister next to him. Across the room, his supervisor Rosa looked up from her newspaper. "Oh what rubbish, Sam! Put that down. There are lots of challenges. Of course chronic conditions are a concern but so is our ageing population. And so is the cost of medical technology. Our Centre is pioneering coordinated care for patients with complex needs… but I guess that kind of news doesn't sell newspapers." Sam put the paper down and sat up straight to reply.

"Sorry, everyone," Shirly bustled in, pushing the door open with an elbow, her hands full of papers. She was the head of the nursing team and a consummate professional. It was unlike her to be late.

Manoeuvring through the mismatched furniture she took a free seat next to Sam and arranged herself at an angle to address the whole room. Normally her laugh filled the clinic and she seemed too vivacious for the stiff neatness of her uniform. But today her face was strained, and she placed her clipboard carefully on her lap.

"Morning everybody," she began, "before handover today, I have two things to say." She waited for everyone to settle down and then looked around.

"Most of you know Mr Williams. Sam, I'm not sure that you've met him: Mr Williams is an 71-year-old man with diabetes, hypertension and early-stage dementia. He's been living on his own, with support from his children who live nearby. Some of you will remember that he was finding it increasingly difficult to control his blood sugar and a couple of months ago blood glucose monitoring revealed abnormal blood sugar levels." Rosa and Anna nodded. "We then started monitoring him with twice weekly blood tests."

"Mr Williams' adherence to his antihypertensive medication was poor – basically because of his increasing forgetfulness – and as a result his blood pressure was not well controlled."

Rosa lifted a finger to signal Shirly. "He always collected his repeat prescriptions on time, but he didn't always remember to take them. His son told me that he has four months of medication stockpiled at home."

"Ah, I didn't know that," Shirly said. She looked at her notes. "Mr Williams is also taking diuretic medication but it seems that he didn't manage to increase his fluid intake at home. Three weeks ago he became dehydrated. I'm sorry to say that this resulted in a fall. His son found him a few hours after he fell and called an ambulance."

There was a pause.

Shirly continued reading from her notes. "From the emergency department Mr Williams was admitted to the acute care ward and treated for dehydration. Due to some initial confusion about who the responsible physician was, two days passed before the orthopaedic specialist was able to review his case."

"On examination the ortho discovered bruising over his right hip and requested an X-ray. X-ray revealed a fractured neck of femur. Mr Williams was put on the trauma list for a hip replacement, with an operation scheduled for the following week." Shirly looked up. "This is about two weeks ago. Is everyone with me?"

Everyone nodded. "After the operation he was transferred back to the acute ward where he made a good recovery and was admitted to the rehabilitation ward. However, during rehabilitation – for his hip – concerns were raised about a cognitive deficit – this would be related to his dementia – and a liaison psychiatric review was requested. After the review it was decided that Mr Williams would not be able to continue living alone and he was discharged to a residential home." She looked around at the group impassively.

"Now it appears that Mr Williams has become increasingly confused and the care home staff are finding him difficult to manage. His GP has decided that access to specialist psychiatric care is necessary and has sent him for readmission."

"So that's why we haven't seen him," Rosa sighed. "That's really a shame. He was doing so well living on his own."

Shirly frowned. "Yes, he seems to have gone downhill very quickly. I'd like to put a group together to think about whether there is anything we could have done differently in his case. Rosa, could you look into that?" Rosa nodded.

Shirly put down her clipboard and fixed her eyes at the back of the room. "Now the second issue today is, well… it's also not good news." She paused and narrowed her eyes. "Dr Mortimer and I had a meeting yesterday. Senior management seem to feel that the Diabetes Centre is no longer financially viable." She looked around the room. "They have initiated a sixth-month review to identify efficiency savings and if those are not found they are considering closing the Centre."

"I don't understand," Asha's voice floated across the room. "Are we losing our jobs?"

Shirly sighed. "No, I don't think it will affect the nursing staff yet. The management team are looking at other services: whether the counsellors are needed, whether we can afford the dietician's programmes, and whether we should continue to run the outreach clinic for early stage case-finding."

"What?" Rosa interjected. "But that will undermine the quality of services we've developed here! We've worked for years to build up early intervention and preventive care."

Asha leaned forward. "What does Dr Mortimer say?"

Shirly picked her words cautiously. "Dr Mortimer appreciates the management's financial concerns and can see no alternative course of action." She knew that vilifying the clinical director might take the pressure off now but would serve them no good in the long run.

Sam picked at the sharp edge of his uniform. He was the most junior nurse and the most recent addition to the team. He had been so thrilled with the job and just last week he had signed a 12-month contract for a studio flat close to the hospital. As a fresh graduate, he would probably be the first one to go.

"Has the decision already been made?" he asked. Even as he spoke his words echoed awkwardly in the room.

Shirly glanced at the wall clock. Patients would be arriving soon.

"Look everyone," she said, her voice rising slightly. "Clearly this is cause for concern and I will make time to discuss it with each of you individually. Right now however, we need to get on with the morning clinic. Remember, patients come first, so put this out of your mind for the moment."

She rummaged in her papers for the handover sheet and launched into the morning routine. "OK, in Chair 1 we're going to have Mr Jonas... Asha, can you take him? ... And we need a stock check... Sam can you do that?"

It was business as usual.

3.10.1.2 The Suggestion Box

But it didn't feel like business as usual. Sam couldn't put it out of his mind. It was the staff who made the Centre so wonderful but now the good cheer was reserved for the patients. The minute they turned away their faces fell. Sam had a feeling that something could be done – that something *must* be done.

"Shirly," he called out, as she swept past the nurse's desk. She turned partly towards him. "Ah, Sam," she said, catching her breath, "What can I do for you?" She was, as ever, in the middle of something else.

"I'd like... I mean... ummm," he paused, and then the words rushed out before Shirly could move on. "Could I create some kind of a suggestions box? Staff might have ideas about how to cut costs in their area and we could share them."

Shirly glanced at him in surprise. "Sure, that's fine. It'll be good to see what the team's thoughts are of course and if there are any useful ideas I'll pass them on to Dr Mortimer." As she turned to go, she looked back at him. "It's nice that you want to help, Sam," she smiled and walked off.

The next day Sam wrapped a shoe box in gift paper and set it at the nurses' station. The red and gold stripes stood out proudly next to the packs of latex gloves and disinfectant wipes. Whenever he passed the station he reminded his colleagues to submit their ideas. At the end of the week the box was stuffed and scraps of paper poked up through the rectangular opening in the top of the box.

From her desk Shirly watched Sam pull up a chair and sit down at the station's computer. He opened the box, pulled out the folded sheets of paper, and smoothed out the creases. Then he leaned forward to read them. She turned her attention back to the towering pile of files in front of her, the interminable paperwork which made her time with patients fleetingly rare.

Name	Suggestion	Sam's Research References
Asha	At a conference last year someone talked about changes they had made on the ward that improved patient care and saved money. I think there are some good practices we would pick up from Operation TLC.	Operation TLC www.globalactionplan.org.uk/
Anna	Until last year I worked in the kidney unit. They made a lot of efficiency changes and I remember hearing that the National Health Service would save £1 billion if their work was rolled out nationally!	Green Nephrology http://sustainablehealthcare.org.uk/sustainable-specialties-greening-nephrology www.bmj.com/content/346/bmj.f588
Rosa	I've been reading about new ways of dealing with anxiety and depression. Some mental health people are talking about how to avoid over-prescribing and non-pharmaceutical treatment options. Maybe there are ideas for us there?	Sustainable Psychiatry http://sustainablehealthcare.org.uk/podcasts/2015/01/3-minute-film-sustainability-mental-health

The following Friday Sam and Shirly walked to an empty Relatives Room to discuss the issues undisturbed. "I don't have long I'm afraid," Shirly said, checking her watch as she sat down, "We've got a ward round at 3pm." She looked at Sam expectantly.

Sam cleared his throat. He arranged two piles of paper in front of him. "The suggestions fall into two categories. First, there is a lot of information about how we run our buildings and the infrastructure of the Centre. I've called that 'Estates Savings'." He pulled up a stapled collection of documents and handed it across the table. Shirly lifted her chin to read.

"For example, we could save money with better waste management or by insulating the building to save energy," Sam began. "We could print less often, now that many of our documents are online."

Shirly took off her reading glasses and smiled widely. "Alright, Sam. It's true that every little bit helps. Initiatives like this can save money, but a few pennies on the pound won't do. We're facing much larger financial difficulties."

"I know, I know," Sam hurried on. "There are other suggestions and all of those savings *together* will help, but maybe not enough. That's why, in this second pile I've put suggestions about the clinical side of things. Ideas for better treatment options, or prevention of illness. I've called this pile 'Clinical Savings'."

Sam handed the top packet to Shirly and watched as she skimmed the pages. "Sum this up for me," she sighed. "What is the main suggestion?"

Sam's eyes widened. "Well it's about the 'triple bottom line'. That means trying to reduce costs, improve patient care, and reduce waste and pollution, all at the same time."

Shirly flipped the pages. "Has this been tested somewhere?"

"Well, that's what's so great," Sam sat forward in his chair. "One hospital ward tried out a project to make operational savings… and they found that it improved patient experience too. It's called TLC." Sam leaned forward to make the acronym clear: "'T' for 'turn off equipment', 'L' for 'lights', i.e., turn them off where possible, and 'C' for 'close doors and windows'. And of course TLC is also short for Tender Loving Care, which is about patients."

Shirly shifted her position on the chair. "Go on."

"In another clinic they improved care quality while reducing both costs and waste just by telephoning patients who had just started on a new drug to see how they were doing. Just a few simple phone calls reduced non-adherence from 16% to 9%! So patients' health improved and that cut down on unnecessary admissions and appointments."

Shirly glanced upwards, lips pursed.

Sam hurried on. "Some projects are getting patients to take a more active role in their own care, treating them as partners. They monitor their own blood pressure. Or they keep an eye out for the side effects of medications, and then increase or decrease their dose. Or they flag up warning signs before complications set in, if they know what to look for." He stopped and looked to Shirly for support. "Would these things work here?"

Shirly nodded. "They might. It's true that if we encouraged telephone and email consultations we would cut down on routine appointments which don't add anything to the quality of the patient experience. But someone will need to go through each of the ideas systematically and get an estimate of the potential savings. And the possible risks."

She looked at the piles of paper. "It would mean quite a transformation in how we do things but it'll need a bit of political will. I'm not sure that there is enough here to convince Dr Mortimer."

"Shirly," Sam leaned forward again. "I was thinking about the patient you told us about, about Mr Williams." Shirly raised her eyebrows and sighed. "Rosa says that as part of his case review we could see whether we could have improved outcomes while also using some of these ideas to cut costs and reduce waste. It would be a test case for these ideas."

Shirly frowned. "Hmmm, that's an interesting idea. Can you and Rosa put together some concrete ideas and get them to me by the end of the week?" She looked at her watch. "And now you should get back to the ward, I'm sure your patients miss you." She winked at Sam, stood up and was out the door before Sam had gotten to his feet.

3.10.1.3 The Proposal

On Monday morning Sam and Rosa sat down with Sam's packet of proposals and Mr. Williams' voluminous case file. "How should we start?" asked Sam excitedly.

"Well," Rosa replied, "I think we should map out all of Mr Williams' experiences. What happened to him? Were any of his problems preventable? What was the cost of not preventing it – to his health and to the health service? What could have been done differently – to prevent his suffering and to save money?" She pulled out a fresh sheet of paper and sketched out a simple grid.

"Yes," Sam replied. How could care be improved and waste be reduced in Mr William's case?"

3.10.2 Case Study: The Seat Belts in School Buses Controversy[10]

∧ N Z Australia &
New Zealand
S O G School Of
Government

On 21 October 2005, a school bus hit a truck and rolled over at Baldivis, about 50 kilometres south of Perth. The accident left 25 teenagers hurt, one critically and four seriously. The bus belonged to a private school, Mandurah Baptist College, and was fitted with sash seat belts. However, the accident was quickly interpreted as highlighting the fact that seat belts were not compulsory in school buses. A flurry of public commentary followed, much of it making the case for compulsory seat belts. The Western Australian government had to respond to this policy issue in the face of intense media and public scrutiny.

3.10.2.1 Children, Safety and School Buses

The Western Australian government, like all Australian state governments, manages a fleet of school buses for transporting students to and from government schools. They are commonly known as 'orange buses'. The buses are privately owned, mostly by small family operators. The state government's Public Transport Authority (PTA) regulates the operation of this fleet and pays the owners for their services. In 2005 the fleet numbered about 800 buses and was used by about 24,000 students. Most of these operated in rural areas. In addition the Education Department owned and operated a fleet of about 150 buses for use in transporting state school students to and from special events. Private schools either owned their own buses or chartered buses from the private sector.

School Bus Services, a branch of the PTA, managed school bus safety, carrying out inspections and enforcing design requirements. National standards for vehicle safety were prescribed by the Australian Design Rules (ADR), administered by the Commonwealth's Department of Infrastructure and Transport under the *Motor Vehicle Standards Act 1989*. ADR 68, concerning occupant impact protection in buses,[11] required all Australian buses to have seat belts, with the exception of public transport buses, buses with fewer than 17 seats, and buses with seat heights lower than a metre. Thus it was the norm for school buses not to have seat belts.

In 2005 Western Australia had a Labor government led by Premier Geoff Gallop. The PTA fell under the jurisdiction of the Minister for Planning and Infrastructure, Alannah MacTiernan.

Labor had won the 2001 state election on a platform that included a promise to trial the implementation of seat belts in school buses. However, the government refrained from action on the grounds that it was awaiting the findings of research on the matter by the

Queensland transport safety authorities. A research report was expected to be published sometime in 2005.

The generally accepted view in both government and the PTA was that seat belts in school buses were a low priority. The previous Coalition government under premier Richard Court (1993–2001) had not pursued the issue. It was widely understood that school buses had a very good safety record, and that the fitting of seat belts would be costly and not the best use of public money even from a children's safety standpoint.

However, this view was not universal. In June 2005 a small advocacy group, the Mosquito Mums, had had a petition lodged in the Legislative Assembly with 567 signatures asking for compulsory seat belts and that no child should be allowed to stand in school buses.[12] The petition was put forward by Labor member for Mindarie, John Quigley. One of the activists, Debbie Diamantis, a British migrant, had memories of a school bus accident in Britain in which 11 children were killed, where seat belts were not being used. Quigley's grievance speech cited two bus accidents in Queensland: one at Mount Tamborine in 1990 in which 18 tourists were killed, and another on the Gillies Highway in 1987 in which six schoolchildren died.

3.10.2.2 The Baldivis Bus Accident and the Public Response

In the first newspaper reports of the Baldivis accident the local police inspector claimed that the presence of seat belts had minimised injuries. This claim was echoed by Debbie Diamantis of the Mosquito Mums group. Murray Cowper, the Opposition spokesperson for road safety, contended that the accident showed that seat belts save lives. The school principal said the same. Labor backbencher Quigley maintained that schools should refuse to hire buses not fitted with seat belts. Rob Fry, president of the WA Council of State School Organisations, was reported as saying that all school buses should be fitted with seat belts.

On Saturday 22 October 2005, the day after the accident, the Director General of the Department of Planning and Infrastructure, Greg Martin, met up with Premier Geoff Gallop at an unrelated event. The two briefly and informally discussed the previous day's accident and Martin advised the Premier that it was the nationally held view that compulsory seat belts were not a high priority in light of the opportunity costs and the safety record of school buses.

The next day, 23 October, the *Sunday Times* newspaper reported Premier Gallop as saying that school buses were generally very safe and Michelle Roberts, Community Safety Minister, as claiming that seat belts were costly and not cost-effective.[13] On the Monday following, the state's rival newspaper, *The West Australian*, reported Alannah MacTiernan as saying that the cost of fitting seat belts could be $50 million, with little safety gain.[14]

Thus the government had a clear and consistent line of argument: the number of accidents involving school buses was minimal, and the cost of retrofitting buses and replacing those which could not be retrofitted was more than $50 million. In addition, a Queensland-based research report was due to be considered in the next month by Australian Transport Ministers. MacTiernan said the research was expected to take the view that only buses on dangerous roads should have seat belts and that buses without seat belts were safer than cars with them.

However, the pressure on the government mounted.

On Tuesday 25 October, *The West Australian* reported that a school bus contractor in Busselton, Ray Gannaway, had been fighting for more than a year for PTA to allow him to get seat belts fitted to three new buses being built for him in NSW, as the PTA were concerned that "premature allocations of buses with seat belts may create a community expectation that if your buses are fitted with seat belts then all buses should have seat belts." Mr Gannaway said that the cost would be an extra $14,000 per bus, or the equivalent of 50 cents a seat each week over the life of the bus contract. Facing criticism from the Opposition and the WA Council of State School Organisations about "bureaucracy gone mad," Minister MacTiernan was reported as saying that she would overturn the PTA ruling, thereby allowing Gannaway to have seat belts fitted, but defended the PTA officers.[15]

On the second weekend after the accident the *Sunday Times* took up the case for seat belts, running a front page and several other full-page stories on the issue. The paper reported the position of MacTiernan and the government, which now was that it would work towards having a "targeted implementation plan" for some buses on identified dangerous routes.[16] But in an editorial it answered the cost–benefit argument with the claim that "$50 million is no small sum, but a price can't be put on a child's life," and in any case the government had a surplus of $1.2 billion. Seat belts could be paid for out of earmarked infrastructure spending or from revenue from stamp duty.[17]

Reporter Joe Spagnolo backed this up with an article entitled "Throw Out Calculator," in which he quoted the WA Government's Office of Road Safety as saying that seat belts in cars reduce deaths by a factor of ten.[18] The paper launched a petition for compulsory seat belts in all school buses. Fry and Diamantis were quoted in support.

On the following Friday, 4 November, *The West Australian* quoted the Police Commissioner, Karl O'Callaghan, as saying that having school buses without seat belts was an "unsafe practice." The safety of children in a crash was "paramount." "I don't think it is a good message to send to young people that they should put on a seat belt in the car but when they are in the bus it's OK not to wear a seat belt," he remarked. Belts should be introduced gradually, including on all buses on which schoolchildren travel en masse. Gervase Chaney, the president of the Kidsafe WA board, commented that "it was astounding that the cost of installing seat belts was considered more important than children's lives."[19] All this was strong support for the *Sunday Times*' position.

On the Saturday, however, despite a recent history of antagonism between the state government and *The West Australian*, the newspaper strongly endorsed the government's stand.[20] MacTiernan was supported as being "on the right track: relevant research must be taken into account and the matter thought through before a decision is made." The benefits of belts were questioned. "There is a strong case to be made that more lives would be saved and injuries avoided if more safe cycle paths were built and underpasses and guarded crossings provided at schools near busy roads."

This point was reinforced in a separate article by journalist Jessica Strutt.[21] She reported the views of Professor Drew Richardson, the NRMA-ACT Road Safety Trust chairman, who was also professor of emergency medicine at the Australian National University. Richardson supported seat belts in buses but argued that it was a lower priority than other measures. He noted that there were 178 road fatalities in WA in 2004, none of which involved buses. "Seat belts in school buses is about priority number six after all the things we should do to get the 178 fatalities down." On his calculations, retrofitting school buses with seat belts "would cost up to $500 million per child's life saved." Strutt added that "WA Public Transport Authority records show that there has never been a child fatality on the State's contracted school bus system. Orange contract buses have been involved in 110 crashes over 10 years, resulting in only minor injuries to just 15 students."

A little over two weeks since the accident, the government was under strong pressure from safety and education groups and the Opposition, galvanised by a campaign from the *Sunday Times*. *The West Australian*, however, had come out in support of the government's policy position that the opportunity costs involved in adopting compulsory seat belts were not worth the benefit, given the safety record of school buses in WA and Australia, and that a Queensland research report would be presented soon which might shed more light and advice on the situation. The political question was whether it was worth holding out against the criticism, in defence of a policy position that seemed to have intellectual merit if not popularity.

3.10.3 Case Study: James Walker and the Line Manager[22]

James arrived at Johannesburg-based St Stephens Solutions, a project management firm, 18 months ago, having previously held roles at two rival organisations, also based in South Africa. He moved to South Africa from Australia five years ago and was keen to broaden his experiences as a project manager, having initially impressed the recruitment team at St Stephens with his recent portfolio of clients, with whom he had successfully been contracted to manage significant construction projects.

He reported to Bryan Pollard, who had been with the firm for more than ten years and who was responsible for a team of seven project managers, including James. At first, James seemed to get off to a good start, picking up new projects and working closely with Bryan and his team to develop project proposals in accordance with the client's demands. The clients seemed to take an immediate liking to James and his rapport seemed to be warm, friendly and positive. However, Bryan soon started to sense that something wasn't quite right as, one by one, the other members of his team began making comments about James' performance. James seemed to be very good at doing exactly what was requested and little more. He tended to find the simplest and most straightforward way to complete a task, rarely doing more than was asked of him, but always taking time to build his own networks and friendships with the clients. In some contexts, this would be fine, but often in Bryan's experience, projects would not go to plan and the team were frequently required to go the extra mile to complete additional work or manage other issues that hadn't initially been anticipated. One by one the team started to make comments back to Bryan suggesting James was avoiding these issues wherever possible, leaving other members of the team to pick up the extra workload. Bryan could sense that tensions were mounting among the team.

As James' line manager, Bryan knew that he would have to call James in for a conversation, but he was also aware that the clients had taken a real shine to him. He was unsure how to handle the conversation.

3.11 IN SUMMARY

In summary, this chapter has:

- introduced you to eight different types of case study, which serve different learning functions and for which some tend to favour specific subject areas;
- compared the merits and pitfalls of drawing insights from field researched cases, desk-based cases (based exclusively on previously published material) and cases derived from the author's general experiences;
- explored different ways that cases are presented to you, with different types of text-based formats and multi-media formats.

NOTES

1 Heath, 2015, p11.
2 Ellet, 2018, p131
3 Mauffette-Leenders et al., 2007, p45.
4 Heath, 2015, p29.
5 Morris, 2022, p1.
6 Adler, University of South California, quoted in Raufflet and Mills, 2017, p4.
7 Schonell and Macklin, 2019, p1197.
8 Elam and Spotts, 2004, p60.
9 Stefi Barna, Emma Pencheon and Aditya Vyas of Medact (United Kingdom), wrote this case based on published sources and generalised experience as part of an Erasmus+ funded programme entitled medicalpeacework.org © 2016. Reproduced by permission.
10 Professor John Phillimore and Alan Tapper from Curtin University in Australia wrote this case study which was produced as part of the Case Program of the Australia and New Zealand School of Government (ANZSOG) and is reproduced with permission © 2013.
11 See www.comlaw.gov.au/Details/F2006L01454.
12 See Hansard, 30 June 2005, pp3758–3759.
13 Flint, J. (23 October 2005) 'Proof School Buses Need Seat Belts; Mothers Lobby for Belts', *Sunday Times*, p1.
14 Penn, S. (24 October 2005) 'Boycott Buses Without Belts: MPs', *The West Australian*, p8.
15 Jerrard, S. (25 October 2005) 'Crash Sparks Safety Row', *The West Australian*, p3.
16 Spagnolo, J. (30 October 2005) "Gallop Avoids the Seat-Belt Outcry. Only Some Buses Will Get Restraints', *Sunday Times*, p10.
17 Editorial (30 October 2005) 'Gallop is Wrong on School Bus Seat Belts', *Sunday Times*, p1.
18 Spagnolo, J. (30 October 2005) 'Throw Out Calculator', *Sunday Times*, p1.
19 Morfesse, L. (4 November 2005) 'Police Chief Wants Seatbelts on School Buses', *The West Australian*, p9.
20 Editorial (5 November 2005) 'Minister Has to Make Best of Safety Money', *The West Australian*, p18.
21 Strutt, J. (5 November 2005) 'Seatbelt Money "Better Spent on Safe Lane for School Buses"', *The West Australian*, p8.
22 This case was originally produced by the author as an illustration of an incident case for Andrews, 2021.

CHAPTER 4

How Do I Analyse and Evaluate My Case?

This chapter will consider three major perspectives for the case: the concepts or techniques that need to be deployed, the analytical opportunities presented by the class, and the manner with which the data and the details are presented within the case narrative. These three combined determine the difficulty or complexity of the case. Often, there is more than one viable approach or response to the case situation, so this chapter explores the skills needed to argue the adequacy of your own analysis and the evaluation of each component of your case.

> As you review [the] cases you will put yourself in the shoes of the managers, analyse the situation, decide what you would do, and come to class prepared to present and support your conclusions.
>
> (Harvard, US[1])

To help make sense of case analysis you might find it helpful to firstly read the Nusr-Et Case Study, which is provided below. You are invited to imagine you have been given this case study to prepare for a class discussion. This chapter will use this as a case example from which to explore many of the principles of case analysis and evaluation, considering how it might be used in the class discussion and how you could draw from management theory to help make sense of the issues raised.

4.1 CASE STUDY: NUSR-ET: SUSTAINING THE PERSONALITY BRAND[2]

DOI: 10.4324/9781003345978-6

When I first started work, I used to say, "I'll strive to be the best in Turkey!" After opening the Dubai restaurant, I said, "The best of the Middle East!" But even I didn't imagine this much. Now being the best in Europe or even the world is within reach! In one and a half months we're opening in Doha, followed by restaurants in London and New York.[3]

(Nusret Gökçe, 22 January 2017)

"So…it's sex," said our dining companion, a meat-and-potatoes Chicagoan, as he wiped his face. Meat juice had squirted onto his cheek during the tableside theatrics… But no, it's not exactly sex. And it's not exactly food either… As a brick-and-mortar meme, it's a miracle. As a restaurant, it's a mess…The staff took the liberty of tipping itself 18%. We left hungry. Salt Bae stayed thirsty. He's on track to drown in his thirst.[4]

(*TimeOut New York*, 2 February 2018)

Nusr-Et may be this season's most-talked-about restaurant, but be warned – it isn't ready yet for prime time, no matter how many likes Salt Bae gets on Instagram… last Sunday night, Nusr-Et was Public Rip-off No. 1. An up-and-mostly down meal for three, where each of us had just one cocktail and one glass of bad wine each, cost a whopping $521.45 – and left us craving a snack.[5]

(*New York Post*, 23 January 2018)

In the backdrop of all the headlines, March 2018 brought the news that a group of major investors, Temasek Holdings[6] together with Britain's Metric Capital,[7] were close to completing the purchase of a minority stake of 17% in the restaurant group D.ream (which included the Nusr-Et restaurants), owned by the Turkish conglomerate Doğuş Holding. The investment group would buy in to 45 brands, 170 restaurants and the extremely popular internet Salt Bae personality,[8] noting the steakhouse chain was being valued at $1.5 billion[9] and highlighted as the most profitable restaurant in the D.ream Group.[10] The initial announcements were enthusiastic, with Metric managers noting they were "excited by the opportunity to participate in the further growth of the company" and "delighted to be partnering with Doğuş and Temasek in this transaction."[11] Doğuş Holding sounded equally pleased, noting that they were happy to bring in new investment from giant companies to Turkey and to have the chance to promote Turkish cuisine and hospitality to the world.[12] Barely four months after the investment, however, there were reports that Doğuş Holding, which co-owned Nusr-Et restaurants, were at odds with its local creditors over the restructuring of nearly €2 billion in maturing debt, only half of the conglomerate's debt woes.[13]

4.1.1 Nusret the Butcher

It was February 2018 and Nusret Gökçe, aka Salt Bae, a 35-year-old bachelor with 13 children, had just moved in the Plaza Hotel in New York, a short distance (which he commuted to on a self-balancing board) to his newest steakhouse Nusr-Et.[14] While he claimed that "The man who does not spend time with his family is not a real man,"[15] his six restaurants and strict personal regimen did not leave time for much else. Sunday mornings started at 6–6.30 am with a glass of water and a cup of coffee and oatmeal before heading to the gym for an hour to an hour and a half. His routine consisted of a combination of combat sports and bodyweight work, "to keep him quick [in the kitchen]," he noted.[16] Breakfast consisted of exactly eight hard-boiled eggs, picked apart to consume just the whites, with very little toasted bread, cheese, and tomatoes.

He donned his usual outfit: V-neck white t-shirt with slim fit black trousers, $600-a-pair dark sunglasses,[17] his hair slicked back. He reminded people of Johnny Depp, while citing Marlon Brando and Al Pacino as his idols.[18] He might have been regarded as a bit too womanish and well-groomed, but he was, after all, nominated as one of the 25 hottest bachelors in New York.[19] "I am a clean man, I pay attention to what I wear. I work in the service sector; it is my respect to my customers," he noted,[20] adding: "I love myself. I want to look stronger and be better. I leave all of the negative energy there and go to the restaurant with more positive energy."[21]

He reached his New York restaurant latest by 9 am. The morning started with a recap of the previous night with the cooks and staff, and Nusret then moved on to preparing the meats for the day. He ate some nuts around 6 pm and had his protein-heavy dinner at 7.00 or 7.30 pm before dinner was served in the restaurant. After that, he did not eat anything at all. He never had any time, anyway, as he visited all the tables and had photos taken with the guests till midnight, when things slowed down. He would be the last to leave the restaurant, usually around 2 am, as a display of leadership to his staff, after listening to a few songs at the bar.[22]

Nusret did his work with extreme pride. He personally "went to meat" to pick the best quality. In photo shoots, he told the photographer to "respect the meat" and reminded the studio staff to hurry up: "I only have half an hour – 200 people are waiting for me."[23] He called himself an artist of butchery: "I cut my meat like poetry, I talk to it, I instill in it my love. Meat is sacred to me. Some men look at a beautiful woman and sigh, 'She must be mine;' that is how I feel when I see meat." Perhaps not surprisingly, his viral videos of preparing his meat were deemed highly erotic.[24]

Working hard and self-discipline were dominant characteristics of Nusret's nature, built up on his innate talent over the years. "I didn't have much of a childhood; I always worked. I remember financial troubles, hardships," he noted. The fourth of five siblings born in Erzurum in Eastern Turkey to a coal miner and a housewife, he decided that further education was not in him after failing 6th grade twice. At age 13, he joined his elder brother who worked at Günaydın Butcher, a well-known butcher shop and restaurant in the Bostancı district of Istanbul. He took the 7 am train to Bostancı daily for a nearly two-hour commute. He worked non-stop, without taking leave or holidays, doing odd jobs, legwork, cleaning, taking orders from 10 different butchers, till he went for military service. He was not even allowed to touch the meat till he was gradually allowed to remove its bones; a move that differentiated between those with a knack for the knife and those without.

> Masters do not like to share what they know; they don't tell you how to do things. You have to learn by yourself, by watching. If you are smart, you pick up the tricks of the trade. And like me, you may begin to love the work. I have been doing this tirelessly for 15 years.[25]

Günaydın had two branches at the time, one focusing on butchery and the other operating as a kebab restaurant. Nusret worked in the former, displaying his talents and establishing good relationships with its customers over time. When the third branch was opened in 2008, Nusret was appointed as head of butchery. The hugely popular restaurant hosted 500–600 people a day. The staff were rushed off their feet but Nusret still found the time to pay attention to the guests' individual preferences, picking, treating, and cooking their meat their way before handing the dish over to the waiters, gaining customer appreciation. Word of mouth soon had it that one should "go to Günaydın and find Nusret." He claimed his popularity was outshining the work of the waiters and chefs, who in turn complained to Günaydın's boss. The boss wanted to send him back to the older branches, a plan that was rejected by Nusret, who had realised the potential of the new branch. "And then they fired me!" Nusret exclaimed. Günaydın managers soon regretted their decision and made Nusret another offer within a couple of weeks. He was appointed to a smaller butcher shop also owned by Günaydın, located across one of Günaydın's larger restaurants. The smaller shop's traffic was insignificant compared to the larger restaurant, which was frequented by customers Nusret knew from the older branch. He started preparing meat for his former customers from his smaller shop and shipping them to the restaurant across the road. At first Günaydın management turned a blind eye, till they noticed that the small restaurant was cannibalising the larger restaurant's sales. Once again complaints flew to the bosses. "You're a butcher, stay as a butcher. You have no business interacting with the customers!" he was told. The brand name of Nusret was getting ahead of the Günaydın name.

At this point, Nusret decided he had to get serious about his career and made a plan to go to Argentina to tap into the world-renowned reputation of the country for meat preparation and cooking. His customers, many of them influential businessmen, diplomats, and celebrities, helped him locate contacts. His bosses were unsupportive. Nusret was not fazed, and took out loans to spend three months in Buenos Aires, working in famous restaurants and watching local butchers and chefs, which resulted in his development of new menu items such as *lokum* (Turkish delight), *kafes* (cage), and *ceviz* (walnut).

A year later, Nusret was convinced he needed to go to New York to observe its famous steakhouses. Despite his bosses' annoyance, Nusret once again used his customers' connections to gain access to Kemal Binici, co-owner of the famous Pasha Restaurant in New York. The US consulate refused Nusret's application three times, before accepting his last application, partly based on the newspaper articles on Nusret's local fame. To his dismay, Nusret discovered that the steakhouse kitchens were dominated by Mexican chefs who had a limited repertoire, consisting mainly of chops and steaks. The learning process seemed to be the other way around, with the Mexican chefs videotaping Nusret's procedures. Kemal Binici, the restaurant owner, informed Nusret that he was inviting journalists that night and told him to "just do his thing." Nusret was in the *New York Times*.

Upon returning to Istanbul, Nusret continued his work at Günaydın. When a large Chinese group that wanted to make a reservation at the restaurant was refused service due to renovations going on in the building, Nusret invited them over to the small restaurant across the road. That was the last straw for the bosses – Nusret was going rogue again. The catalyst needed to launch the Nusr-Et story had just been sparked.[26]

4.1.2 The Nusr-Et Story

Nusret Gökçe's first restaurant, Nusr-Et, opened in 2010 in Etiler in Istanbul[27] with support from his partner, Mithat Erdem. It soon became a great hit among celebrities and business folk. A 40-minute wait for a table became the norm at this restaurant, which did not have much ambience and served only meat, salad, and potatoes. Nusret could be seen behind the barbecue smoke, personally cooking the meat and serving it to his customers, many of whom he addressed by name and knew their preferences. Particularly after the famous Turkish gourmet Vedat Milor visited the restaurant and announced it on television as the best steakhouse in Istanbul,[28] Nusret the butcher was raised to legendary status at the age of 28. His modest looking restaurant became the place to see and be seen, and visitors queued up to have his rockstar charisma reflected in a selfie. His unusual way of sprinkling salt, which he called his "last touch that blesses the meat,"[29] became his signature act and turned into a viral sensation.[30]

By the end of 2011, it was announced that Ferit Şahenk, main shareholder and Chairman of the Board of Doğuş Holding,[31] the eighth richest man in Turkey and also a customer of Nusret's restaurant, had paid US$6.8 million for a 50% stake in Nusr-Et.[32] In 2012, Nusret was invited to the Dominican Republic set of *Survivor*, a reality TV competition show hugely popular among Turkish audiences, where winners of a certain stage of the game got to watch Nusret perform his butchery and cooking show and later taste his special meats.[33] He went on to become a regular on this show, making Nusret a household name. January 2013 saw the opening of a restaurant in Ankara, the capital city of Turkey,[34] followed by Marmaris on the Aegean coast, in April 2014.[35]

Nusret's international expansion abounded, and in December 2014 Nusr-Et's Dubai restaurant opened its doors, neighbouring other well-known restaurants. With no PR promotions, opening day hosted 500 people, with phones ringing off the hook and people standing and waiting for 2–3 hours for a table despite having reservations. The first week continued with a full house, with Nusret working very hard and meticulously to feed 600–700 people a day.[36] In three months, 6,000 people had been served at Nusr-Et Dubai.[37] The Abu Dhabi restaurant followed in 2017,[38] once again packed with Arabs, mobile phones ready for a snapshot of the star in action,[39] or if that was not possible, just a selfie in front of the Nusr-Et sign at the entrance. The princes of Dubai and Abu Dhabi became regular Nusr-Et customers.[40,41] By 2017, Nusret Gökçe's YouTube followers had reached 2 million; he had 7 million followers on Instagram, and famous talk shows mentioned him all over the world.[42] "If I didn't have a language problem, I'd accept all the advertising offers coming in from everywhere!" he exclaimed, somewhat surprised at the amazing interest he had garnered as a one-man international Turkish brand. Meanwhile, Nusret was invited to the Laureus World Sports Awards ceremony in Monaco as a surprise guest of honour and his presence was announced with a tweet including his photo and the statement, "Well Well Well! Look who salted the #Laureus17 Red Carpet."[43] He later appeared in the promotion video of the third series of the Colombian Netflix TV series *Narcos*.[44] His social media nickname of #SaltBae stuck, and his fame reached even new heights as Rihanna was seen wearing a T-shirt with a drawing of Salt Bae conducting his famous salting move,[45] David Beckham and Justin Bieber tried the move on camera,[46] DJ Khaled and Drake were taped salting Nusret's freshly cut meat,[47] WNBA player Angel McCoughtry named the salted caramel and chocolate variety in her ice cream parlour Salty Bae, Danny Welbeck from Arsenal mimicked the move to celebrate a goal,[48] and celebrities like Leonardo di Caprio, Puff Daddy, Dr. Oz[49] were seen being served in his restaurants.[50]

But the massive popularity did not detract him from his ambitions, which kept increasing in scale.

> When I first started I used to say, "I'll try to be the best in Turkey!" After opening Dubai I said, "The best in the Middle East!" But now the situation calls for the best in Europe, in fact, the world! But I need to work harder. My main job is not the show, it's the meat. I got this far because I was good at the meat. But it's not enough to be just good anymore. We live in such a world that the work you do has to have a story. You have to sell the story, you have to mesmerize the people, grab their attention. All of us have to create a brand from ourselves. There's no bread for anyone otherwise![51]

While being aware of the criticism he attracted from competitors for his flamboyant showmanship, he did not let it get to him: "They say I'm not refined enough. Brother, I'm the son of illiterate parents! I've worked harder than a whole lifetime of the people who gossip about me, and I'm still working. I'm 34; where I've come to in 20 years is not bad, really!" About his social media popularity, his reflection was that his theatrical meat cutting and salting act, performed without input from agents and PR professionals and recorded on phone cameras by whoever among the staff is free, was not only skilful, novel, spontaneous, and interesting, but it also portrayed a man presenting an aura, a persona, and who could actually make fun of himself.[52]

The 2018 international expansion plans included Doha, London, and New York,[53] but many other cities were cited as potential locations, including Miami and Dallas, with Nusret's intriguing reputation preceding any potential restaurant launch.[54] Meanwhile, the second restaurant in Kanyon Shopping Mall, Istanbul, was announced in April 2017;[55] a restaurant in Bodrum (on the Aegean coast of Turkey) opened in June 2017,[56] and Nusr-Et Burger, the fast food line of Nusr-Et, started operations in the Bebek, İstinyePark, Kanyon, and Nişantaşı locations of Istanbul over the summer of 2017.[57]

4.1.3 "If I Can Make It There..."

Nusr-Et's US adventure started with a 250-seat restaurant in Miami in November 2017, serving 1,000 meals a day.[58] The New York restaurant, seating 150 with an outdoor area of 80, opened its doors in January 2018 in Manhattan.[59] The opening weekend critiques were overwhelmingly negative.[60] Joshua David Stein's description of his experience in GQ did not hold back:

> When the Salt Bae arrives it is like death. One knows one must die and yet the moment it comes is still surprising... Is the steak transcendent? No, the steak is mundane, somewhat tough and rather bland. The hamburger is overcooked. The tartare is over-chopped. The cocktails are terrible and the water... is $9... It does not matter. In a world where nebulous social media influencers get paid thousands

of dollars for a post, is it really absurd to pay a mere $500 for Salt Bae to slip into our feed? No, it is human. And humans are idiots.[61]

Adam Platt from Grub Street concurred, while noting the amount charged – $745 for two:

> Did I pay much attention to the chalky quality of my mashed potatoes after the star of this strange show moved on to sprinkle his digital fairy dust over the next table, and the table after that? Did I complain bitterly about the tomahawk, which, when compared to Manhattan's other, more robust versions of this already ridiculously hyped dish, was a little puny and roughly 100 percent overpriced? Not really – why would I? As other critics have pointed out, Nusr-Et is more of a theatrical happening than a real restaurant, and like it or not, we are all part of the show.[62]

Robert Sietsema from Eater, New York, commented that $320 for two, with service automatically included and the diners leaving still hungry, could only be justified if one appraises the place as a dinner theatre, adding, however, that after having seen Nusret's show many times before, one feels the play needed a second act.[63] This would be tough to achieve, however, noted Lauren Steussy from the *New York Post*, as the more restaurants Nusret opens, the fewer tables he can visit. She added:

> from the looks of the lunch crowd and their apparent disregard for the cost of their meal, it's clear they want one thing: Salt Bae, tableside, holding that pose a second longer so they can get the angle right on their phones.[64]

Pete Wells from the *New York Times* agreed:

> Much as I enjoyed meeting an obliging human meme, I was distracted by unwelcome thoughts all night. The most annoying one was money... One day, the prices will stay behind while Mr. Gokce leaves New York to salt other steaks and other laps. Without him, the dining room will be even stranger than it is now.[65]

Steve Cuozzo from the *New York Post* was harsh, calling the restaurant "underwhelming" and "Public Rip-off No.1," while adding: "We want more substance with the smoke and salt – and dishes that not only sultans can afford."[66]

Clayton Guse from *TimeOut New York* was ruthless:

> This year, New York welcomed the grand sultan of suckers: Salt Bae...The establishment may very well be the greatest con to be pulled off in New York City... The food is bad. The experience of Salt Bae emphatically cutting a steak barehanded in front of you is somehow sexual and certainly perturbing. For some, spending that much money for an Instagram post is worth it. But for most New Yorkers, it's more like throwing a rent check out the window... Salt Bae is simply selling bullshit. He's co-opted a self-promoting meme into something that might as well be a bank heist. Considering that Salt Bae has more than a dozen restaurants across the world, his presence in his midtown dining room will not be permanent... Nusr-Et is not worthy

of New York City's restaurant scene, but it's what we deserve. We all helped create this monster… What we're left with is a world where a truly terrible steakhouse can thrive in a coveted Manhattan location, and it needs to be stopped. If we want to keep calling New York the greatest city in the world, it's high time we stop wasting it on terrible, uninspiring people and products… [D]ear New Yorkers,… let the Salt Baes collapse into the sodium-filled pits where they belong.[67]

Richard Morgan from *TimeOut New York* calls the restaurant "a mess," criticising, among other things, the wait staff's lack of expertise,[68] an issue also brought up by Pete Wells.[69] While later reviews noted that some of the earlier complaints had been alleviated, the upsell had not changed.[70]

"You want to hate the place, to dismiss it… Yet, when Salt Bae shows up to slice and season our steak, it's embarrassingly thrilling, like watching your favorite cheesy movie," admitted Kate Krader[71] from Bloomberg.

Meanwhile Nusr-Et's Miami restaurant was not faring any better. An Instagram photo of a cigar-smoking Nusret paying homage to Fidel Castro soon after his death drew thousands of irate comments from Cuban-Americans vowing never to eat there.[72] Jodi Mailander Farrell from the *Miami Herald* noted that without Nusret's presence they were "left with salty stand-ins, watered-down cocktails, and a breathtaking bill." She had visited the Miami restaurant twice over two months and noted that the food was not enough to entice her back:

Without Salt Bae on site, Nusr-Et is just another steakhouse (and a very expensive Instagram photo). It will take more than a viral flick of the wrist for it to survive in this town.[73]

Nusret, having recently been featured on NBC Television[74] and the *Dr Oz Show*,[75] shrugged off the criticisms, saying, "It's been a full house since we opened. That is my only performance criteria. I'm here to stay."[76] However, it looked like he had got the message: It was rumoured he was doing market research for a private jet so as to travel more easily between his restaurants.[77]

4.1.4 Trouble Ahead?

While Nusret Gökçe felt he could handle the critics, a new threat to his new restaurant appeared. Just days after the opening of the New York restaurant, *Eater* magazine suggested that Nusret's bare hand contact with the meat and his wearing of accessories (in this case, his large gold watch) were violations of article 81 of New York City's health code, upon which the Department of Health initiated an investigation.[78] Nusret was later seen using a glove for his salt sprinkling move, though people noted that the salt was still touching his forearm.[79] This minor offence did not detract from the hype that followed the announcement of the London Park Tower Knightsbridge Hotel restaurant opening[80] and the launching of Salt Bae, the hamburger chain spinoff for Nusr-Et, in Los Angeles[81] and Soho.[82]

In May 2018, Nusret Gökçe opened a new restaurant in Istanbul's famous Grand Bazaar, the opening ceremony being attended by numerous celebrities,[83] bringing the number of

Nusr-Et branches to seven. A wax figure of the famous butcher was unveiled in July 2018 to be placed in the newest branch.[84] This latest launch was somewhat shadowed, however, by Nusr-Et's large advertising billboard on the historic gate of the bazaar being slammed by many users as an "insult to history" and "insolence," resulting in its removal and a fine being issued by the municipality.[85] Later, in September, a video posted of Venezuela's President Nicolas Maduro eating at the new restaurant and Nusret carving meat with dramatic flair for the president and his wife, were quickly deleted after international outrage.[86] Less than a month later, Donald Trump Jr. was ridiculed online by people appearing to be President Trump supporters disheartened by his son posting a video of himself being served by a chef who had recently served a "socialist dictator."[87]

While being acknowledged as a world-renowned Turkish brand at this point,[88] challenges still awaited Nusret Gökçe and his restaurant chain, Nusr-Et. With a major Turkish conglomerate backing him, his restaurant chain had expanded rapidly both in Turkey and abroad, stretching Nusret the persona to his limits. New York had been less than accommodating to the steakhouse's assertive and somewhat ostentatious entry into the market. And now the international investors that had taken a share of the restaurant chain were in conflict with its local partners. Nusret himself was well aware of what could happen: "The service sector is like no other. You present and serve great food for 364 days. One day you're in a bad mood, something's happened, and people say, 'Nusret, I didn't like this at all... You've gone bad!' The 364 days go down the drain because of that one day."[89]

Would Nusr-Et's global operations be sustainable, given that its major investors in and outside of Turkey were running into financial conflict? How sustainable would a one-man show be, solely relying on the talent and charisma of Nusret Gökçe? How would the New York experience affect the success of other launches in major cities around the world? It seemed that the investors had a lot to consider.

4.2 ANALYSING THE CASE STUDY

The same preparation for case discussion, which was detailed in Chapter 2, should apply to this case prior to its delivery in the class for a group discussion. From your analysis of this *desk-based* case (which draws insights from previously published material) you should immediately notice the broad range of 100 references used to inform the narrative and which therefore demonstrates that there is a lot of online content available on the issues of this case if you were to choose to explore online as part of your preparations. This part of the chapter considers how the case might be used in a class setting.

The authors had anticipated that the case could be used as a discussion vehicle with which to begin an exploration of issues involving celebrity culture, marketing/PR, and strategic decision-making. The case can also be used in Brand Management classes to discuss brand-building processes, primarily for a discussion of the application or implementation of symbolic branding strategies. It is written in such a manner to make sure it could be used for both MBA and undergraduate Business Management, Marketing, and PR programmes. While purposely devoid of credible quantitative financial data, it may be used to trigger a wide range of issues and questions for discussion.

Remember, at the beginning of this chapter, it was suggested there are three major perspectives you should consider when preparing for a case class discussion: the *concepts or techniques* that need to be deployed, the *analytical opportunities* presented by the class, and the manner with which the *data and the details are presented* within the case narrative.

Concepts and Techniques

So, what are the concepts or techniques that could be deployed for this case? Well to begin, it is important to consider the objective of the case study, which for this Nusr-Et case is to evaluate the model adopted by Nusr-Et (or Salt Bae) to deliver a sustainable steakhouse restaurant chain with multiple sites in major cities across the world, while being highly shaped around the persona of one individual.

The case invites you to examine the role of publicity in brand development and, in particular, to consider the function of persona branding and the role of celebrity culture.

While some publicity may appear to be negative, it reconsiders the popular question of whether all publicity is still good publicity. Given that the case also draws attention to the role of investors and other stakeholders, you may be invited to consider the perspectives of different stakeholders in this case and to explore the issues raised from different stakeholder viewpoints, to comment on attitudes and behaviours that impact on decision-making, and to explore issues of operational capacity and strategic decision making.

From a branding perspective, the case aims to make students recognise the importance of the consumer and market in the strategic brand-building process, and your tutors might choose something like the application of the *brand resonance model* to help examine this.[90] The case also provides opportunities to evaluate various symbolic branding strategies[91] according to the benefits the symbolic brand provides to different markets.

Analytical Opportunities

Having explored such concepts and techniques, the next step is to consider the analytical opportunities presented by the class session. The author's intention in leading the case discussion is to encourage students to challenge traditional views and conceptions of Marketing and PR in contrast to more contemporary approaches of informal branding and celebrity/personality branding. The case also provides an opportunity for management decisions to be evaluated both from the perspective of Nusr-Et and its future investors.

There are many ways in which discussions on the case can be opened. Prior to the class you may have been encouraged to investigate and explore data available online that relates to the Nusr-Et story to inform the case discussion, commenting on the impact of celebrity endorsements and noting the negative reviews that have also been widely published (there is a lot of content out there). Links to many of these are provided in the case study. The case discussion could be shaped around one of two key themes:

1. The role of celebrity publicity and the concept of personality branding; or
2. The pros and cons of investing in a global concept like Nusr-Et.

The case discussion could begin by first identifying the target market for the brand and to consider whether it is a *symbolic* or a *functional* brand. You should notice that from a branding communications point of view there are at least two markets in which Nusr-Et is operating. The domestic Turkish market and the US market are the ones for which the case provides the most information, so the customer profiles can be defined for these two markets. The brand knowledge established in the minds of the consumers (associations of the brand) varies a lot for these two markets. You might be asked to delineate these associations and assess if they relate to the aim of the brand as a status marker providing authenticity.

The case depicts how a brand is formed through various practices that are not always very strategic but rather guided by an entrepreneurial spirit. Therefore, with careful facilitation from a trained case tutor, you should be able to evaluate this brand formation process through a strategic brand management perspective and be able to locate how the brand formation process follows the resonance model (which includes development of awareness, performance and imagery, thoughts and feelings, and resonance levels). Thus, you may be invited to comment on:

- How awareness is created and the activities that lead to awareness formation in different markets.
- How performance/quality perceptions are formed in different markets, and how brand imagery develops through communications.
- The attitude towards the brand in two different markets.
- Being a symbolic brand, whether the brand manages to form a strong emotional relationship with the customer.

Presentation
Having considered the *concepts or techniques* that could be deployed, and the *analytical opportunities* presented by the class discussion, then the third perspective you should consider is the manner with which the *data and the details are presented* within the case narrative.

The Nusr-Et case has very limited financial data and has intentionally incorporated many quotes from a broad range of different sources, so it is quite likely that you will be required to provide some form of synopsis of these comments, which you might then be asked to draw from to offer a novel strategy to build and sustain this symbolic brand.

To help makes sense of this, here is a list of questions that you could be asked during the class discussion session, which are grouped around three themes:

1. What are you learning about the role of celebrity publicity and the concept of personality branding?
   - What are the distinguishing features of the Nusret Gökçe brand?
   - In what areas could the Nusret Gökçe brand be improved?
   - How dependent is Nusr-Et on Nusret Gökçe?
   - How dependent is Nusr-Et on the celebrity culture?
   - What are the keys to a successful personality branding concept?
   - Is this a fad or a sustainable concept?
   - What is the impact of negative publicity on personality branding?

- How does Nusr-Et manage its customers to encourage repeat purchases?
- What lessons could Nusr-Et learn from other successful restaurant brands?
- What lessons could other successful restaurant brands learn from Nusr-Et?
- What does the story of Nusr-Et teach us about informal brand communications?

2. What are the pros and cons of investing in a global concept like Nusr-Et?
- Given that the business environment in Turkey is not entirely positive as the parent company of D.ream is facing a debt crisis, what do you think of Temasek's decision to invest in D.ream?
- How can medium- to long-term planning be considered when looking to invest in concepts like Nusr-Et?
- How are risks identified, appraised, and managed in such investment considerations?

3. What is your evaluation of their present branding strategy, and could you consider implementation of an alternative strategy?
- Evaluate the current brand building strategy of Nusr-Et. Does the current process fit with the brand resonance model? Why?
- What is the main benefit of this brand to its customers?
- Discuss the branding strategies that can be applied to successfully create and sustain Nusr-Et.

4.3 CASE DIFFICULTY

Having looked at the concepts or techniques that might be deployed, the analytical opportunities presented by the class, and the manner with which the data and the details are presented within the case narrative, it is reasonable to conclude that the same case study could be used several different ways and delivered to different levels of difficulty or complexity. Often, there is more than one viable approach or response to a case study situation, so your tutor will no doubt select an approach based on your prior experiences and anticipated developmental level within the programme you are studying. I have been known to select the same case study to use with first-year undergraduates, final-year graduates and postgraduate students, but the approach I take (or put another way, the journey I require the student to take through the case data), and the manner with which we treat the case data will differ for all three groups. This adaptation of the case method according to difficulty or complexity is helpfully summarised by Mauffette-Leenders, Erskine and Leenders, who were originally based at the Richard Ivey School of Business in Canada. They developed a *Case Difficulty Cube* as a widely quoted model to evaluate approaches to case study delivery. Figure 4.1 illustrates the model demonstrating that difficulty is a product of concepts, analysis and presentation.

If you and your student group are relatively new to the case method, then it is unlikely you will be expected to undertake highly complex analyses of case data in the first instance. Sometimes, a case tutor might provide details about a particular concept or theory prior to starting the class case discussion, or occasionally, there might be a pause in the discussion to allow the tutor to provide a 'mini-lecture' to introduce a model or theory that

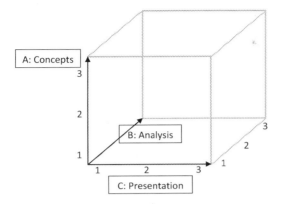

FIGURE 4.1 Case Difficulty Cube

Source: J. David M. Wood, Michiel R. Leenders, Louise A. Mauffette-Leenders, James A. Erskine (2019), *Writing Cases*, (Fifth Edition) pp 15–22. Reproduced with permission.

you might then continue to use and to apply as part of the ongoing case discussion. Your tutor may adopt a more directive teaching style in your early case sessions whereby they might work through examples of case exercises with you to demonstrate how you could approach a certain task. In time, the tutor will then look to be less directive, enabling you to take the initiative with such exercises.

To *manage pace* in a case class discussion it is quite common for tutors to assign tasks in-between discussion points and to invite you to form small groups to discuss the tasks and then feedback what you have undertaken to the larger group. These so-called *breakout groups* ensure you and your peers remain on-message as participants in the case discussion rather than bystanders. If you are required to tackle a particularly complex concept or dataset, then it is likely that you will have more extended periods of time in breakout groups to ensure you have rigorously considered all aspects of the task you have been set, before feeding back to the main group. It is also quite common to undertake polls or quizzes as part of the case discussion process, as this further supports your engagement and also demonstrates to you the likely breadth of opinion among your peers about the subject matter that you are exploring.

4.4 DEVELOPING YOUR ARGUMENT

Finally, when you are preparing your case analysis one final word of advice is to ensure you have built sound argumentation into your analysis. If you are required to provide a decision, some form of analysis, or recommendations, then it is important to ensure your responses are grounded in good argumentation. Toulmin produced a helpful model to make sense of sound argumentation, which is commonly used today as it breaks down your argument into six components: claim, grounds, warrant, qualifier, backer and rebuttal.[92] The three main parts of the argument are the *claim* (the point you are trying to make that you want others to believe), the *grounds* (the data, evidence or basis upon which you are locating the claim) and the *warrant* (the logical assumptions that connect

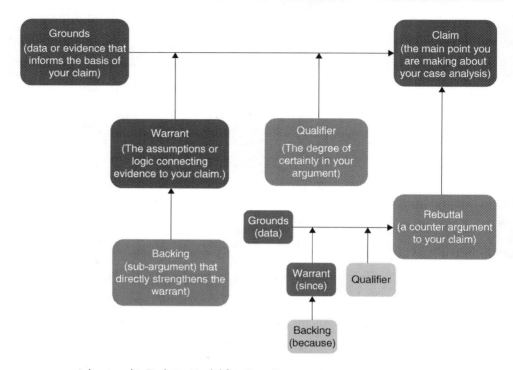

FIGURE 4.2 Adapting the Toulmin Model for Case Discussions

your grounds or evidence to the claim). In addition are the three minor parts of the argument, which include the *qualifier* (this is normally some form of statement which shows how convincing or strong your claim might be), the *rebuttal* (this is the counter argument or an opposing point of view about your claim), and the *backer* (additional reasons that you might draw from to support the warrant). While there are many interpretations of this model in literature, Figure 4.2 provides a simplified view of how to set-out your argument using this Toulmin approach.

4.5 IN SUMMARY

In summary, this chapter has:

- introduced you to approaches that are likely to be adopted during the class discussion including application of concepts or theories, analysing case data and working with different types of data presentation;
- provided a *worked-through* example of how a tutor could use a full case for class discussion;
- delivered insights into how to build your own argument when making a claim in defence of your case analysis.

NOTES

1 Hammond, 2002, p1.

2 S. Nazli Wasti, Middle East Technical University and Scott Andrews, University of Worcester, wrote this case based on published sources. Data collection was supported by Merdan Tokdemir and Deniz Demircioğlu. Reproduced by permission. ©2019

3 www.hurriyet.com.tr/yazarlar/ayse-arman/avrupanin-hatta-dunyanin-en-iyisi-olacagim-40342837

4 www.timeout.com/newyork/restaurants/nusr-et

5 https://nypost.com/2018/01/23/theatrics-cant-save-salt-baes-leathery-130-steak/

6 Investment company headquartered in Singapore owning a large portfolio of businesses in Asia.

7 An independent private capital group that invests in European small and medium sized businesses.

8 www.verdict.co.uk/salt-baes-restaurant-investment/; www.hurriyet.com.tr/ekonomi/d-reame-singapurlu-ve-ingiliz-ortak-40799695

9 www.thenational.ae/business/salt-bae-restaurant-chain-valued-at-1-5bn-1.711576

10 www.sabah.com.tr/yazarlar/kadak/2018/07/22/dogusun-dreami-3-yildir-krini-yuzde-100-buyutuyor; https://businessht.bloomberght.com/piyasalar/haber/1866573-nusr-et-in-sahibine-yeni-ortak-mi-geliyor

11 www.metric-capital.com/announces-investment-in-dream-international/

12 www.hurriyet.com.tr/ekonomi/d-reame-singapurlu-ve-ingiliz-ortak-40799695

13 www.bloomberg.com/news/articles/2018-04-16/salt-bae-diner-s-owner-said-to-start-talks-on-2-5-billion-debt; www.hurriyetdailynews.com/salt-bae-fined-for-insulting-shop-sign-at-istanbuls-historic-grand-bazaar-134916; www.sozcu.com.tr/2018/ekonomi/reuters-dogusun-borc-yapilandirmasinda-surec-uzuyor-2511624/; www.theonlinecitizen.com/2018/07/25/barely-4-months-after-temasek-invested-millions-in-turkish-restaurant-chain-its-parent-conglomerate-is-facing-severe-debt-restructuring-woes/

14 A play on words: 'et' means 'meat' in Turkish. https://mobile.nytimes.com/2018/02/16/nyregion/how-salt-bae-restaurateur-spends-his-sundays.html?referer=https://www.google.com/

15 www.ladbible.com/more/viral-salt-bae-shows-off-his-nine-kids-in-instagram-post-20170212

16 www.menshealth.com.au/get-ripped-like-salt-bae

17 https://nypost.com/2018/01/23/theres-more-to-salt-bae-than-steak-and-seasoning/

18 www.hurriyet.com.tr/yazarlar/ayse-arman/avrupanin-hatta-dunyanin-en-iyisi-olacagim-40342837

19 https://nypost.com/2018/07/21/the-25-hottest-bachelors-in-new-york/

20 www.hurriyet.com.tr/yazarlar/ayse-arman/avrupanin-hatta-dunyanin-en-iyisi-olacagim-40342837

21 https://mobile.nytimes.com/2018/02/16/nyregion/how-salt-bae-restaurateur-spends-his-sundays.html?referer=https://www.google.com/

22 Ibid.

23 www.hurriyet.com.tr/etlerin-efendisi-19579308

24 www.youtube.com/watch?v=nci1nFzB36o

25 www.hurriyet.com.tr/etlerin-efendisi-19579308

26 Ibid.

27 This restaurant moved to a nearly location, also in the Etiler district, in June 2012. The former location continued operations as a butcher shop.

28 www.youtube.com/watch?v=-b3ZxYkEJpU

29 www.hurriyet.com.tr/yazarlar/ayse-arman/avrupanin-hatta-dunyanin-en-iyisi-olacagim-40342837

30 www.ladbible.com/more/viral-salt-bae-shows-off-his-nine-kids-in-instagram-post-20170212

31 Major Turkish conglomerate with over 120 firms and around 30,000 employees at the time.

32 www.sabah.com.tr/ekonomi/2011/12/25/sahenk-steak-kral

33 www.tv8.com.tr/survivor/gonulluler-muthis-odule-kavustu-nusret-onlari-ete-doyurdu-12602-video.htm

34 www.gecce.com.tr/haber-nusr-et-steakhouse-ankarada-aciliyor

35 www.alpertekbas.com/haber/datcada-cennetten-bir-vaha-236.html

36 www.milliyet.com.tr/nusr-et-dubai-yi-fethetti/magazin/ydetay/1989490/default.htm

37 www.sabah.com.tr/yazarlar/sinan-ozedincik/2015/04/05/seyhler-nusrette-siraya-girdi

38 http://abudhabieats.com/nusret-abu-dhabi/

39 www.hurriyet.com.tr/yazarlar/ayse-arman/avrupanin-hatta-dunyanin-en-iyisi-olacagim-40342837

40 www.sabah.com.tr/yazarlar/sinan-ozedincik/2015/04/05/seyhler-nusrette-siraya-girdi

41 www.hurriyet.com.tr/yazarlar/ayse-arman/avrupanin-hatta-dunyanin-en-iyisi-olacagim-40342837

42 www.youtube.com/watch?v=nci1nFzB36o

43 https://tr.sputniknews.com/spor/201702151027220443-sporun-en-iyilerinin-aciklandigi-torende-turkiyeden-surpriz-konuk/; www.youtube.com/watch?v=BmIyyherDNM

44 www.ntv.com.tr/sanat/narcos-3-sezon-icin-nusretli-tanitim,9bdVrU2eZkaopSjZnPE43w

45 https://twitter.com/nusr_ett/status/823426121639358468

46 www.elle.com/uk/life-and-culture/culture/news/a41170/brooklyn-david-beckham-saltbae-impression/; https://london.eater.com/2018/1/31/16950446/salt-bae-nusret-steak-restaurant-london-knightsbridge

47 www.vladtv.com/article/238191/drake-and-dj-khaled-put-finishing-touches-on-salt-baes-work

48 https://london.eater.com/2018/1/31/16950446/salt-bae-nusret-steak-restaurant-london-knightsbridge

49 https://nypost.com/2018/01/23/theres-more-to-salt-bae-than-steak-and-seasoning/

50 www.ladbible.com/more/viral-salt-bae-shows-off-his-nine-kids-in-instagram-post-20170212

51 www.hurriyet.com.tr/yazarlar/ayse-arman/avrupanin-hatta-dunyanin-en-iyisi-olacagim-40342837

52 www.hurriyet.com.tr/yazarlar/ayse-arman/avrupanin-hatta-dunyanin-en-iyisi-olacagim-40342837

53 www.qatareating.com/%E2%80%8Esaltbae-nusret-sheraton-doha/

54 www.newyorker.com/culture/likes/the-chef-who-sprinkled-some-joyand-salton-2017

55 www.akilligundem.com/nusr-et-yeni-subesini-kanyon-avmye-aciyor/

56 www.cokertme.com/haber/nusr-et-steakhouse-bodrum-palmarina-subesi-ile-yeni-sezona-hazir-8808.html

57 www.geccemekan.com/haber-nusr-et-burger-uc-yeni-noktada-misafirlerini-agirlamaya-basladi; www.fdmagazin.com/haber-19963-nusret_gokce__istinyepark_avmde_acildi.html

58 www.turkavenue.com/index.php?option=com_content&view=article&id=5061:nusret-new-yorktan-sonra-miamide-aciliyor&catid=102:basari-hikayeleri&Itemid=643; https://emlakkulisi.com/nusr-et-miamide-4-kasimda-aciliyor/551339

59 www.nytimes.com/2018/01/12/dining/salt-bae-nusr-et-openings.html?action=click&contentCollection=Food&module=RelatedCoverage&region=EndOfArticle&pgtype=article

60 https://nypost.com/2018/02/04/salt-bae-to-open-burger-chain-in-nyc/; http://time.com/5119654/salt-bae-restaurant-bad-reviews/

61 www.gq.com/story/salt-bae-nusr-et-review

62 www.grubstreet.com/2018/02/adam-platt-salt-bae-nusr-et-steakhouse.html

63 https://ny.eater.com/2018/1/22/16919590/salt-bae-restaurant-nyc-what-to-order; www.independent.co.uk/life-style/food-and-drink/nusr-et-salt-bae-new-york-city-reviews-cost-price-a8176311.html

64 https://nypost.com/2018/01/23/theres-more-to-salt-bae-than-steak-and-seasoning/

65 www.nytimes.com/2018/02/02/dining/salt-bae-pete-wells-nusr-et-steakhouse.html

66 https://nypost.com/2018/01/23/theatrics-cant-save-salt-baes-leathery-130-steak/
67 www.timeout.com/newyork/news/you-created-salt-bae-and-now-you-have-to-eat-his-nasty-food-020618
68 www.timeout.com/newyork/restaurants/nusr-et
69 www.nytimes.com/2018/02/02/dining/salt-bae-pete-wells-nusr-et-steakhouse.html
70 www.bloomberg.com/news/articles/2018-02-01/salt-bae-nusr-et-review-new-york-s-most-controversial-steakhouse
71 www.bloomberg.com/news/articles/2018-02-01/salt-bae-nusr-et-review-new-york-s-most-controversial-steakhouse
72 www.miamiherald.com/entertainment/restaurants/article205300579.html
73 www.miamiherald.com/entertainment/restaurants/article205300579.html
74 www.youtube.com/watch?v=6xU78SFQBjE
75 www.hurriyet.com.tr/video/dr-oz-showda-nusret-ruzgari-40749164
76 www.hurriyet.com.tr/kelebek/hurriyet-pazar/nusr-etin-saltanati-bitti-mi-yoksa-yeni-mi-basliyor-40723140; https://nypost.com/2018/02/04/salt-bae-to-open-burger-chain-in-nyc/
77 www.milliyet.com.tr/nusret-ucak-aliyor--magazin-2700906/
78 https://nypost.com/2018/01/31/health-codes-are-cramping-salt-baes-style/
79 www.sozcu.com.tr/2018/dunya/nusr-ete-kotu-haber-new-yorkta-sorusturma-aciliyor-2197500/
80 https://london.eater.com/2018/1/31/16950446/salt-bae-nusret-steak-restaurant-london-knightsbridge
81 https://la.eater.com/2018/6/7/17438136/salt-bae-nusret-gokce-opening-los-angeles-arts-district-burgers
82 https://nypost.com/2018/02/04/salt-bae-to-open-burger-chain-in-nyc/
83 www.hurriyet.com.tr/kelebek/magazin/yeni-sube-kapalicarsida-40832430
84 https://metro.co.uk/2018/07/22/salt-bae-reaches-legend-status-gets-wax-figure-now-seen-7745192/?ito=cbshare
85 www.hurriyetdailynews.com/salt-bae-fined-for-insulting-shop-sign-at-istanbuls-historic-grand-bazaar-134916
86 www.bbc.com/news/world-latin-america-45559504
87 www.indy100.com/article/donald-trump-jr-salt-bae-nusret-gokce-restaurant-nicolas-maduro-instagram-new-york-8582281
88 www.youtube.com/watch?v=WS7J2XeKa6I
89 www.hurriyet.com.tr/yazarlar/ayse-arman/avrupanin-hatta-dunyanin-en-iyisi-olacagim-40342837
90 The brand resonance concept is from Keller, 2013.
91 For example, see Rosenbaum-Elliott, Percy and Pervan, 2015.
92 Toulmin, 2003.

CHAPTER 5

So What?: How Has the Case Helped Me to Learn?

Any case study delivered in a classroom context ought to be contributing something new to your *learning*. But how do you capture this, evaluate its impact, and ensure this *learning* is 'stored' in such a way that enables you to reutilise the learning derived from the case in future experiences? At the heart of a case study is a *story* and, as one commentator once stated, "we don't listen to stories, we join in," and in accompanying the players of that story we meet many sides of ourselves. This chapter examines the heart of the case discussion process by considering its overall contribution to our learning. First, let's look at what others have had to say about the way in which the case method contributes to your learning:

> Actively apply what you are learning in your own, specific management situations, past and future. That will greatly heighten relevance. Even better is to pick a situation that you know you will face in the future where you could productively use some good ideas.
>
> (Harvard, US[1])

> Cases are to management students what real bodies are to medical students – an opportunity to practice harmlessly.
>
> (Richard Ivey School of Business, Canada[2])

> Integrating e-learning technologies such as discussion forums with the traditional case method pedagogy has the potential to change educational processes and enhance the quality of learning in this environment. Combining online discussion forum and case study analysis offered students a high-quality learning environment.
>
> (Sydney Business School, Australia[3])

It is worth noting that these three quotes refer to applying what you have been learning into your own context, practising repeatedly and discussing with others. These three themes will be developed further in this chapter, beginning with logging and applying what you have learnt.

DOI: 10.4324/9781003345978-7

5.1 APPLYING WHAT YOU HAVE LEARNT

As I mentioned earlier in this book, one of the areas I find myself challenging my students about most often is to think independently: to foster curiosity, ask awkward question and delve deeper into the management issues they encounter. This often starts by asking the *so what?* question. In the US this is often referred to as the *takeaways* from the case class discussion. While each case study provides an insight into a particular management issue located in a specific organisation, the ultimate task of the case study is not to develop your skills as a master of that specific management issue for that specific organisation. Asking the *so what?* question enables you to develop your thinking further and then to transfer it into other management contexts; or as one commentator put it, "to take the learning back to my real world once the playing is over."

I completed my MBA almost 30 years ago and while most of the management content of that programme has become well-grounded in my day-to-day thinking these days as a scholar of management, the most memorable of those MBA sessions are firmly located in specific class case study discussions. I can still remember the case studies that my tutors gave me – the titles of the companies and the issues they were facing. Since those days, as a case tutor for more than 25 years, I am most encouraged when I meet up with a former student who relates in some detail a specific management issue that they have recently faced in their workplace, and in attempting to work out a solution to the situation, they were able to draw parallels from earlier class case studies and use these to transfer the learning into their current workplace context. This transferable learning lies at the heart of the *so what?* question.

The *so what?* question is what brings the *reflective practitioner* out of you. There are plenty of papers that draw attention to the importance of *reflection* as a key component of learning, alongside *input learning* and *discovery learning*. We all learn in different ways and not all of us are natural reflective learners, but there is little doubt that developing skills of reflective practice will improve our capacity to learn, to transfer learning and to recall past lessons-learnt that we can apply into new contexts. I can personally testify to this as I know that I am not a naturally reflective person. Most self-perception tests will testify that I am activist/pragmatist and that is reflected in my preferred learning styles, but that doesn't stop me appreciating the importance of reflective practice enough to want to do something about it. For me, this has meant building intentional reflection into my pattern of learning, often supported best when I invest time in developing some form of learning log. A typical learning log can be developed in many ways and there are plenty of digital resources to help and support you in developing one that best suits your context. My learning logs tend to include the following questions:

- What is the issue that I have encountered/experienced?
- What did I learn from that experience?
- What do I need to do now in response to this experience?
- What might I do differently next time I encounter a similar situation?

- How does this experience link to other things I might be encountering (either now or in the near future)
- When do I next need to review this log?

You will note that these questions are similar to those attributed to Kolb's experiential learning cycle that was discussed in Chapter 1. The additional points to note here are that I immediately seek to link the experience to other experiences to explore whether the learning from one might provide a better foundation for managing the other. I also make a scheduling decision to ensure I set a calendar appointment for revisiting the experience. This repeated reviewing of the notes from my learning log entry serves to further embed the reflective learning derived from the initial experience.

Case study-based programmes often provide more than one opportunity to encounter any specific type of subject theme or discipline to ensure that not only is the experience noted once but that, through *revisiting*, it can be reinforced in future case sessions.

Your case tutors may develop other techniques to ensure your case discussion is converted into learning experiences including the setting of written coursework inviting you to reflect on the class case discussion and to write-up such reflections as part of a case exercise. This is common practice in many case-based programmes and may even contribute to your overall assessment. Alternatively, you might be required to provide some form of individual or group presentation of your assessment of the case study including your lessons-learnt. These approaches are discussed further in Chapters 10 and 11.

5.2 PRACTISE REPEATEDLY

The case class discussion is not simply there to develop a greater understanding of a particular management situation or discipline. It is also about ensuring you are developing the types of skills that are required in modern management and able to deploy these confidently. Any skill requires repeated hours of practice in order to perfect it. One view of practising for skill development was popularised by Malcolm Gladwell's book *Outliers*, which stated that it takes 10,000 hours of intensive practice to achieve mastery of complex skills.[4] This is a bold and controversial statement, and while others have disputed this claim. it does at least reinforce the notion that *practice makes perfect* and, as such, skill development is something that can be cultivated over time with repeated case experiences. The case method deployed as a regular part of your management programme will enable you to test and develop many management skills that you will likely need to call upon in future workplace contexts, some of which were listed in Chapter 2 and others might include:

- Positive, creative thinking
- Persuasiveness/sharpness
- Metal agility and risk-taking
- Balancing intuition with analysis
- Humility in interaction with others
- Critical mindset

None of these skills, along with those of decision-making, handling assumptions, building argumentation and active listening, can be taught from a textbook or traditional lecture, because they require nurturing and developing. Ensuring you are actively engaging with the case method provides one of the strongest opportunities to develop such skills in management, which is testimony to why the case method has been an enduring practice in so many business schools. Furthermore, as a reflective practitioner, you could practise retrospectively reviewing these lists of skills after each case study to ask yourself which of them have been tested and developed in that specific classroom experience, which ones could have been developed further with greater engagement, and what different actions you might take next time to ensure you are even better predisposed to developing these skills further?

A final thought: don't worry if you trip up during a case study discussion. At first, the case method may not feel entirely comfortable for you. Remember, as the Ivey quote at the beginning of this chapter suggested, a case class is *an opportunity to practice harmlessly*, so reflect positively on your experiences, note any changes you might wish to make for next time and then draw a line under any negative experiences and commit to having another go next time. Over time, I am confident that you will reap the benefits of more positive experiences and you will grow in confidence as you develop your management skills with the case method.

5.3 DISCUSSING WITH OTHERS

We can therefore conclude that learning from case studies can take place both during the class discussion (synchronously or in real-time) and after some reflection on the overall experience of the case, which might be referred to as asynchronous learning. Furthermore, there is no doubt that the learning process is more than just the consequence of bilateral discussions between yourself and the case tutor. One primary purpose of developing the case class discussion is that it puts you into contact with many other opinions and viewpoints from your peers and as such there is a sense of collaborative learning as you effectively support one another in the learning process. Heckman and Annabi put it this way: "The purpose of case study discussions is to allow each student to help other students in the class gain a new perspective on case events."[5] Their research has investigated the ways in which you learn when working in face-to-face (synchronous) classroom case study discussions and when working in asynchronous learning environments (which are particularly pertinent when looking at approaches to online case study learning, as will be discussed further in Chapters 8 and 9).

They explored research that supports the benefits of learning in technology-mediated contexts and the processes for supporting online collaborative learning, while recognising the merits of face-to-face peer learning. Heckman and Annabi argue that the ways in which you collaborate in these two contexts is different and therefore the process of learning is also different. It is recognised that there are normally many 'roles' adopted by students in a face-to-face learning environment compared to an online environment and so these 'many roles' contribute in different ways to how you and your peers will learn. Then, they go further to consider the different roles you can play when communicating with peers in an asynchronous online context. Arguably therefore the authors draw attention to the benefits that can be derived from both online and face-to-face learning and suggest that a combination of these may be a best-fit approach to overall enhanced learning through the case method.

One generalisation from this is to note the importance of your contribution to the benefit of the learning derived by others as well as for yourself. Put another way, if you are not in the classroom and participating in a class case discussion then not only are you limiting your own learning opportunities but also those of your peers, who may otherwise have benefited from your contributions, formed by your unique perspective on the case.

The significant role of peer-to-peer learning has led to the development of pre-case class discussion *syndicate group* sessions being developed in curriculum by some established case programme providers. In these scenarios, students are given the case study in advance to prepare individually in readiness for classroom discussion. Then, on the day of the class discussion, students first meet in scheduled syndicate groups to share their ideas and pool their resources ahead of then moving to the whole class discussion time which would be facilitated by the case tutor. These syndicate groups tend to be student-led and may be steered by a selection of guiding questions provided in advance by the case tutor. This is another example, along with *breakout* groups, of how peer-to-peer student discussions can play a vital role in your learning process.

5.4 IN SUMMARY

In summary, this chapter has:

- introduced you the concept of developing learning logs to support active reflective practice;
- explored ways in which such logs could be used to help reflect on developing essential management skillsets for future case sessions;
- examined the importance of student peer-to-peer learning as one component of the case learning and development process.

NOTES

1   Hammond, 2002, p1.
2   Mauffette-Leenders, Erskine and Leenders, 2007, p4.
3   Seethamraju, 2014, p9.
4   Gladwell, 2009.
5   Heckman and Annabi, 2005.

CHAPTER 6

How Can I Learn through Multi-media Cases?

Traditionally, the case method evolved as a paper-based learning resource, and its popularity continues as such today. However, there are a growing number of non-paper-based case studies that are available in different media formats, many of which are proving very popular with students, who themselves often tend to engage better through technology-enhanced, multi-media approaches to learning. The first challenge here is to ensure that while the format has changed, your role as an active, participating student at the centre of a multi-media case doesn't become passive and disengaged. On the contrary, working with multi-media cases normally offers you the opportunity to take the driving seat as you craft your own journey through the complexities of the case data. This chapter explores the benefits and pitfalls of working with different multi-media case technologies and considers a range of strategies to maintain your active engagement.

> The case method is built around the concepts of metaphors and simulation. Each case is a description of a real business situation and serves as a metaphor for a particular set of problems… Management is a skill rather than a collection of techniques or concepts. The best way to learn a skill is to practice in a simulation-type process.[1]

According to data by The Case Centre on their bestselling case studies of 2021, almost 20% had some form of video or digitally based software embedded as part of the case. While learning platforms change frequently, which may necessitate changes in digital case structuring and design, there can be no denying that there is a growth in digital or multi-media case studies and some business schools and professional digital content developers have emerged over the past 20 years to become pioneers in this field. For the purposes of this chapter, I have chosen to separate these into two distinct categories: video cases and web-based cases. Video cases will be cases that are principally delivered in the form of one single video and web-based cases will include all other multi-media cases that deliver content in a variety of formats on some form of digital platform.

6.1 VIDEO CASES

There are some video cases that are a collection of short videos compiled together to form one unique case study. Most often, these types of case studies may also include a small document with explanatory notes to guide you as you work through the videos. However,

DOI: 10.4324/9781003345978-8

most video cases simply comprise one single video. Your challenge as you work with this video is to remain actively engaged with the content, making notes throughout, rather than viewing this as a passive visual experience.

To help explore this further, this section includes a link to a video case study which explores a groundbreaking expedition to the summit of Everest.

The *Everest! Are You Ready?* case study was developed by Burçak Ozoglu a case scholar and member of the expedition team. The video provides extraordinary, vivid insights into how a national team worked together, often against considerable odds, with the goal to reach the summit of Mount Everest. If successful, this would achieve a number of 'firsts' for the expedition team including:

- the first Turkish national team ascent to the summit of Mt. Everest;
- the first Turkish female ascent to the summit of Mt. Everest;
- the first ascent from Turkey to be made without the help of supplemental oxygen.

Perhaps not surprisingly for an expedition of this nature, not all elements of the project schedule go to plan and so this case explores the challenges of effective teamwork and leadership that are required to manage change in hostile and complex circumstances. One member of the 12-person team became ill at over 8,500m and had to climb down to the advanced base camp. Further complications arose and some members of another team died attempting a similar climb. Three other members of the Turkish team also suffered health issues and needed to retreat, while others had to withdraw from the unmasked element of the trial. The team leader was faced with several difficult decisions as the safety of the team, the progress already made, and the motivation of the team-spirit all played a part in the ongoing decision-making process.

The video of this case study can be found at www.youtube.com/watch?v=zfUqn vs2iV02[2]

This case study provides very vivid insights into teamwork, decision-making, leadership, risk management and crisis management. The author proposed that the case could be used to consider a number of questions and challenges including:

- Prepare a timeline of events, starting from the day the team left base camp.
- What are the main elements demonstrated from the case that contributes to group identity and the characteristics of being a team?
- How might you define teamwork? Was this a successful expedition team or a lucky group of friends?
- What aspects of effective leadership are showcased from the expedition and how does this contribute to your understanding of effective leadership patterns and multi-dimensional decision-making?
- Given the issues and problems raised during elements of the expedition, what could be the factors that provided the required strength and motivational will of the team members to continue?
- Why do you think the expedition leader decided to continue despite all the difficulties and risks? Do you think going on the expedition was the right decision?

As you click on the link to view the video case, it is helpful to be armed with all these questions in advance as they provide reference points for you to ensure you are actively listening and engaging with the video content, rather than simply watching the story unfold in a passive manner. If, however, time permits, then I would recommend watching the video in its entirety first, and then watching it a second time with a pen in one hand and a finger from your other hand on the pause button to take notes to address these questions.

A video case doesn't negate the need for a classroom discussion but rather presents the case data in a different format for you to analyse in readiness for a class discussion. A well-prepared case tutor will then most likely refer to short clips from the full video as part of their facilitation of the case class discussion.

6.2 MULTI-MEDIA CASES

Cases developed on various digital platforms follow similar rules to those described in previous sections. The difference here is your navigation through the case data. Often these platforms will be structured to hold a range of different elements of data to inform the overall case. Your challenge, in the lead-up to a class discussion, will be your careful journeying through all the case content to extract the relevant data. When cases of this nature are presented with multiple file links (a little bit like a buffet with lots of items to choose from), the temptation is to short-cut your preparation and to miss out various elements of the data, but this can prove costly as it is unlikely you will develop a full picture of the situation under investigation. Unlike a single paper case, you are in charge of the journey through these files and so you will normally find you can navigate you route through the case data files in whichever order you choose. Often these types of cases can include text files (for example, reports), organisational charts, images, logs, excel data files, short video clips, email entries and other types of media file.

One further development from the multi-media case is the *simulation case*, which is growing in popularity as it often aligns with the gamification of the case method. This type of case is slightly different to that described above as the structure of the case invites you to particulate in a range of decisions, leading to various 'levers' being pulled to enable you to progress to the next stage of the case. You are effectively given a role within the structure of the case and have to make decisions in order to achieve a predetermined set of organisational objectives. For example, this could be about formulating approaches to acquiring sufficient buy-in from various internal stakeholders to support a change management intervention by choosing specific actions from a range of options. The choices that you make in terms of which levers (decisions) to prioritise will impact your progress through the case, albeit most often these types of cases permit more than one attempt.

Simulation cases are highly complex and require a lot of buy-in and preparation both on the part of the tutor and the students if they are to provide a meaningful opportunity for learning. The priority for you as the student is not simply to enjoy the challenge of performing well in the exercise itself but also to ensure you have fully reflected after the simulation is completed and to ask the all-important *so what?* question. From my experience of integrating these into programmes over the past 20 years, they have proved to be hugely popular with students and tend to be their most favoured case experiences when it comes to student evaluation and feedback.

6.3 IN SUMMARY

In summary, this chapter has:

- explored approaches to engaging with video cases;
- provided you with access to a full, complex video case with questions to help you navigate your way through the video content;
- provided guidance when working with multi-media content on digital platforms to navigate your own journey through often complex case data;
- explored good practice when engaging with simulation case studies.

NOTES

1   Shapiro, 1984, 1.
2   Burçak Ozoglu, wrote this case based on field research as part of an Erasmus+ funded programme entitled Case-Study Alliance Turkey © 2018. Reproduced by permission.

CHAPTER 7

What is a Live Case?

Live cases provide an exciting and dynamic context from which you can explore key facets of management by quizzing individuals from an organisation when they join your group to bring their own insights of a particular management challenge that the organisation is facing. This chapter explores how you can make the most of a live case opportunity, to develop your skills of enquiry, evaluating and decision making, from which to provide valuable feedback to the case organisation as well as preparing you for future management roles.

Here's what others are saying about the merits and approaches to using live case studies, noting the contribution that this type of case study makes to your ability to apply theory, to think critically and to develop team management and communication skills:

> Live case studies are a form of "work integrated learning" (WIL), an umbrella term for student centred, structured education strategies that facilitate the integration of academic theoretical knowledge with experiential knowledge gained in practice contexts.
>
> (Tasmanian School of Business and Economics, Australia[1])

> The live case study was completed at the "host" organization in Sweden and participants travelled from the UK to take part. Prior to the start of the case individuals were given a briefing which provided details on the objectives of the exercise, advice to attend to the process along with the task and a recommendation to devise team rules.
>
> (Ashridge Business School, UK[2])

> The use of live case studies in business education is growing. Mixing realism entices students to think critically in an unpredictable environment. Live cases are often deemed appropriate for international business and strategic cases.
>
> (University of Guelph, Canada[3])

> Students responded that as a result of participating in this project, they had gained confidence in their own ability to apply what they learned in a company setting. The integrative live case experience allowed students to apply marketing concepts, team management skills, and business communication skills.
>
> (Western New England College, US[4])

DOI: 10.4324/9781003345978-9

A live case needs to be treated quite differently to the previous types of case study explored so far in this book as the nature of the class discussion is somewhat altered by the fact that the person representing the organisation at the centre of the case study will be in the room with you.

7.1 COMMON APPROACHES

A live case study normally involves a representative from the case organisation (often a senior manager) coming into class to present a dilemma about their organisation for which your help is required. This is a much more dynamic learning environment as the organisation's representative will not necessarily have made a firm decision yet about the situation that requires actions in their organisation, so your role (and those of your class peers) is to assist the visiting case speaker to determine the company's next course of action and/or response to their situation. This might require various levels of interrogation on your part to ensure you are fully informed with all the data you need to be able to make recommendations. Often a written case report will be provided which may be handed out in advance, to be used as part of your case preparation, setting the scene for the challenge that the visiting speaker will bring to your live case session. Your case tutor will no doubt have already agreed an approach to outlining the case with the visiting speaker and the session might begin with some form of introduction and interview between the guest and the tutor before you are then invited to ask any further probing questions to gather the necessary details to enable you to form a response. Sometimes, the procedure of the live case session might then involve you and your peers forming breakout groups to discuss your various potential responses to issues raised by the speaker before feeding back; or, on other occasions, you may be set group work to complete in advance of either a returning visit by the guest speaker or a report to be submitted for review by the case organisation. As one US professor using live cases pointed out:

> When students know they have to defend their choices to a real client, there is a level of ownership and involvement with the process that I've never seen students express otherwise.
>
> (Marquette University, US[5])

The case class discussion time is therefore very different to that which you would normally expect with any other type of case session. Normally, a case tutor asks a range of questions to enable you, as students, to navigate your way through the analysis of case data to a point where you are able to make some form of judgement, conclusion, recommendation or decision. In a live case, you are the ones often doing the *question-raising* to elicit as much detail as possible from your visiting speaker. So, in a live case, it is imperative that you have already done your research into the organisation before your guest arrives and that you have curated the right types of questions to ensure you gain access to the data you need to formulate a response.

7.2 PREPARATION FOR A LIVE CASE

As already indicated, preparation is key if you are to make the most of a live case study scenario. The consequences of not being prepared are either prolonged awkward silences when you have nothing to raise with the business leader who has given up their time to attend your case class, or worse still, to raise poorly considered, inappropriate questions that demonstrate your lack of awareness about the organisation. This type of case enables you to develop key management and consultancy-type, investigative skills which you can deploy to make a difference for the organisation at the centre of the case. But to do so requires you to adopt a certain mindset for the task that lies ahead. One set of student expectations was outlined by two US-based live case tutors:

The students are expected to do the following:

- Read material, watch videos, research about the case outside of class.
- Apply what they have learned, in class assignments.
- Collaborate in teams, with different class members each week.
- Understand the basic adult learning theory, where they are ultimately responsible for their own learning.[6]

While this is not an exhaustive list, it demonstrates the importance of your preparation. In this specific live case exercise, students were exposed to a real-life restaurant situation, based in Arizona. Students were assigned a number of tasks which culminated in a set of presentations to the restaurant owners which were initially recorded as part of a 'live' presentation at the end of the semester.

If you have the opportunity to present your own questions to the case organisation's guest representative, it is helpful to consider how you might formulate these questions in advance. Raising the right types of questions enables you to achieve a variety of different objectives, as indicated in the examples listed in the table on the previous page.

Question	Orientation
What is the problem here?	Problem identification
How do you feel about...?	Attitude/opinion eliciting
What do you notice about...?	Attention drawing
What other examples are there?	Thought provoking
What might be done to?	Problem solving/reducing
What else might be done?	Generation of alternatives
Would you do that?	Personal preferences
What would be the 'cost'?	Proposal evaluation
What would you do?	Identification

In another example of a live case project, based at a Canadian university, students were invited to design a strategy for a Canadian company to enter the Chinese market. For this particular case exercise, it is interesting to note that before commencing on the live case, all student participants were required to sign a confidentiality agreement to safeguard the sensitive information that the company would be sharing. The student team that provided the most favourable response to the competition were then sponsored to travel to China to develop their ideas further and offered internships with the company. Final presentations were made to the organisation three months after the initial CEO visit, to allow students time to gather data and consider options.

From these examples, it is clear that live cases require a high level of ongoing commitment on the part of the student, often over a prolonged period of time. This does, of course, reflect how such projects often evolve in real-life scenarios, so it is fitting to suggest a live case does provide a very dynamic slice of reality, but this can sometimes be challenging especially if you have been used to working in smaller bite-sized projects that require less agility and shorter periods of engagement. Undoubtedly, this approach to learning with live cases will enhance your employability skills, ensuring you are work-ready as well as developing your understanding of management systems:

> In class, students learn about abstract business concepts. But when a company visits and lays out a specific problem – like how to restructure its incentive program – students are suddenly put inside the business. They must develop different solutions and strategies, think about their implications, and then apply real performance and sales numbers to see how their proposed solutions affect salaries and compensation rates.
>
> (Ohio University, US[7])

7.3 IN SUMMARY

In summary, this chapter has:

- compared the differences between live cases and conventional case studies;
- invited you to think about the processes and approaches that you might need to undertake to ensure you are prepared for a live case class;
- explored different levels of expectations set by tutors for students when participating in live cases with different organisational expectations.

NOTES

1 Schonell and Macklin, 2019, p1197.
2 Culpin and Scott, 2012, p568.

3 Charlebois and Foti, 2017, p1400.
4 Elam and Spotts, 2004, p59.
5 Jessica Ogilvie, quoted in Rapp and Ogilvie, 2019.
6 Green and Erdem, 2016, p44.
7 Rapp and Ogilvie, 2019.

SECTION B

Using Cases for My Online Classes

Even before the global Covid-19 pandemic, there had been a growth in the adoption of case study classes for online programmes. Given the implications of the pandemic in the educational sector and the need to temporarily shift learning to online platforms, there has been significant developments in our understanding of how to adapt our use of cases for online learning, both when delivered in real-time (synchronous) virtual classes and when developed for asynchronous online programmes – where the tutor and the students are not engaging in the case at the same time. This section unpacks the many ways in which these fresh insights have informed the way that case tutors and students are managing learning through online case delivery today, starting with a chapter that focuses on synchronous delivery and then a second chapter that focuses on asynchronous delivery.

DOI: 10.4324/9781003345978-10

CHAPTER 8

Using Cases for Synchronous Online Learning

The recent shift to online learning due to the Covid-19 pandemic has led many case tutors to explore ways of managing case delivery for online programmes in both synchronous and asynchronous formats (and sometimes a blend of both). Since the initial pandemic lockdowns, many business school programmes have continued to offer online or hybrid programmes that incorporate case study learning though online platforms. This chapter explores the adaptations that you may need to undertake when transitioning to real-time (synchronous) online delivery and the potential new contributions to learning that online case delivery can provide.

> An online case discussion can be similar to an underwater video of a starfish colony. At regular video speed, the starfish move slowly and seem solitary, but speed up the film and you will find that they have a lively, if slow, interaction – and are quite social animals.
>
> (Bentley University, US, and the Norwegian Business School[1])

> From Netflix to social media to dishes piling up in the sink, you'll be faced with many distractions that can easily derail your studies. The best online students know how to lessen these distractions and set aside time to focus.
>
> (Northeastern University, US[2])

> Interactive case studies are extremely useful in online training. You can embed links to reference materials, appendices, and detailed figures. Instead of boring blocks of text that most people will overlook, these links can be hypertext, pop-up boxes, or video annotations. You can spice them up by including audio prompts, animated visuals, memes, and GIFs.
>
> (eLearning Industry[3])

Given that "online case teaching is an area that evolves rapidly (mostly because the software tools and learning environments do),"[4] this chapter has avoided focusing on specific online platforms or tools as there will undoubtedly be more in the marketplace as global engagement with online learning continues to grow. Instead, the focus is on how to adapt your approaches and techniques to using cases for online learning.

DOI: 10.4324/9781003345978-11

8.1 INITIAL CHALLENGES

Earlier pre-pandemic studies have identified a number of factors that can inhibit your engagement with online learning, with typical student barriers including administrative issues, lack of social interaction, inadequate technical skills, poor motivation, inadequate time and support for studies, cost, access to the internet, and technical problems.[5] Your programme leaders and IT support services ought to be putting in place all the technical and organisational support you need to mitigate against these challenges, but it is helpful to approach this as a 'joint venture' where you too can put checks in place to ensure you are ready and able to engage with the online case studies that are being scheduled for you. This includes ensuring you have access to the right equipment with the right platforms to be able to access the case content and that, where possible, these have been checked by yourself in advance (to familiarise yourself with the navigational tools). In addition, you need to think about managing the time needed both to prepare for class and to log-in with sufficient time to be ready for the case to begin (bearing in mind that sometimes systems crash or lock you out requiring you to log-in more than once).

Further inhibitors such as boredom, working with silence, feelings of being lectured to (rather than participating), external (off-screen) distractions and feelings of being invisible have also been found to hamper online case delivery.[6] If your experience of using the case method through online delivery is to be impactful, then these typical inhibitors need to be addressed as part of your online case strategy. The next section explores potential responses to these factors.

8.2 ESTABLISHING YOUR GAME PLAN

> Having cameras on also helps with reading nonverbal cues, which are helpful in virtual classroom settings. Encourage students to use thumbs up or down, facial expressions, and gestures to communicate. Eye contact is equally as important – it shows students that you're actively trying to engage with them.
>
> (Harvard Business School, US[7])

Real-time remote learning does come with challenges, particularly as the *technology platforms* required to support engagement are commonly inconsistent and unreliable in different contexts. We've all experienced how it feels to be there 'in the room' one minute and then in the next minute being logged out, freezing, or at best communicating with a constant time lag between participants, which creates a space which is sometimes then filled by several respondents attempting to share at the same time. All this can cause frustration and confusion and in the midst of this, it is easy for you to become distracted. The first thing for you to do is to ensure you have freed yourself from any distractions, that you are in a quiet location, where your bandwidth is likely to be sufficient to sustain the online meeting, and that you (and all the class group) are agreeable to exercising a little patience, as the pace of delivery is unlikely to be the same as it would be if you were meeting face-to-face.

Too many unmuted participants can lead to echoing effects or feedback received over the headphones, so you are likely to be encouraged to mute when not commenting and use the *hand-raise* option to facilitate group chat, but this unavoidably impacts the natural rhythm and flow of a discussion, especially when you are midway through the delivery of your response before realising you have forgotten to unmute yourself (we've all been there!). Ultimately, this draws attention to the emotional energy that you need to reserve for a case class.

These days it is easy to find yourself set up with multiple screens and other devices around you, ready to enable you to find distractions that hamper your overall engagement with the case itself. These are, however, tools that can be used for your own good. If, for example, you are being guided by your case tutor to apply a specific theory or model in your case scenario, it is easy to draw from these other sources to access further details of this model to help inform your ongoing engagement with the case. Similarly, multiple screens mean that you can have one screen that focuses on the class group – the images of the tutor and other peers – while your case data and/or pre-planned notes can be located on other screens.

With these challenges in mind, it helps to set realistic expectations for yourself. Working remotely can easily tire people, and it is likely that you will need a break in-between sessions and some form of disengagement, if you are then to be re-energised to move onto the next session. Students have commented on the value of activities such as a walk around the block, stretching and other exercises, which have been found to provide therapeutic opportunities for students, enabling them to refocus on their forthcoming session.

It is quite easy to see the online environment as a place of shadows within which to hide, but I would challenge you to see it as a place from which to shine. One of the advantages of online case sessions is that they create a more even playing field compared to face-to-face sessions, where quite commonly some of the most confident students might dominate a class discussion. Your tutor's careful management of the online group environment should ensure you can share your own insights within a more equitable teaching framework.

Some cases work better when delivered online and others may be delivered slightly differently online to how they might have normally been delivered in a face-to-face context. Multi-media cases, such as those discussed in previous chapters, which have been devised with online delivery in mind, may prove popular choices, but you need to check that any bespoke digital platforms allow content accessibility on your system.

Some established practitioners of remote and distance learning case sessions believe it is helpful to think more modularly in terms of delivery. While a face-to-face session might support a fluid conversation covering three or four different themes in parallel, an online session often tends to focus on one issue, theme or takeaway at a time.

There is likely to be more polls, more quizzes, more breakout groups and more breaks when working in an online context compared to the face-to-face class. Polls and quizzes keep you connected and engaged with the core issues of the case, while breakout groups provide greater opportunities to ensure everyone contributes, and additional breaks build space or redundancy into the class session, providing vital opportunities for students that are less confident with online learning to catch up. Taking regularly breaks is an important antidote to online fatigue and burnout.[8] Breakout groups are particularly valuable in larger classes, fewer students can fit onto one screen and so it's easier for individuals to feel lost in the shadows, which may subsequently lead to fewer active participants; so be prepared to work harder in the breakout groups and ensure the findings of the group are fed back in the main group session, using the online 'chat' function where appropriate too.

Researchers have noted that where online discussion involves more than around 40 participants, then the nature of the discussion changes. One of the benefits to online case discussions is that you can incorporate different approaches to the other participants' responses, as research from Ivey Business School has identified that:

> in addition to live discussion via video, asking for written responses or comments on posts encourages all participants to think about their responses and show that they are actively engaging.[9]

When delivering a case session in a face-to-face class, tutors are often looking at the body language of their students to pick up cues that can be used to facilitate the conversation. Body language is a less obvious communication tool when participating in online classes so it is helpful to ensure you have your camera on (where bandwidth permits) so the tutor can at least recognise facial expressions and draw on these when facilitating the discussion.

One of the other benefits of an online class is the use of chat boxes, running alongside the main discussion which enable those that might feel less confident to initially engage with the vocal discussion to provide a secondary text-based commentary. This does, however, create an extra layer of complexity for you during the class discussion as it might mean that two separate discussions are happening simultaneously – the vocal discussion or debate and the text-based chat. Keeping an eye (and an ear) on both of these communication flows will help you to fully immerse yourself in the case discussion process. Remember, a well facilitated case discussion is not a bilateral collection of conversations between the tutor and each student, but also a multilateral conversation between all students too (see Figure 8.1), so don't assume that a comment arriving in the text chat is awaiting a tutor's response, it is quite likely that you and others could provide equally meaningful responses to the text chat too.

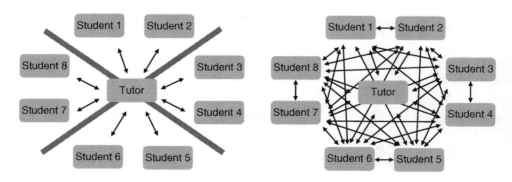

FIGURE 8.1 Multilateral Approach to Case Discussion

Sometimes other communication tools are incorporated into the online case discussion (depending on the technology available), such as the inclusion of digital sticky notes, shared interactive digital whiteboards, and multi-group screen-sharing. All these activities are designed to ensure you have every opportunity to engage with the discussion, and often these resources provide opportunities for subsequent *screenshots* that allow you to capture and take away some of the findings for further reflection (for example, when required to provide a post-discussion, individual, written case report).

In summary, Bixler et al. proposed a three-step framework for tutors to use when integrating case studies for online learning that draws on some of the themes previously discussed, and which are abridged in the following table:[10]

Individual student preparation, leading to...	... Collaborative learning, progressing to...	... Individual student synthesis
Provide video/audio recordings, written materials, etc. for students to learn basic background	Use 'class time' for synchronous or asynchronous active learning including group work, data collection and data analysis.	Encourage higher order thinking and synthesis of learning through additional questions or activities
Use quizzes or other activities to hold students accountable	Ensure all students are engaged in specific tasks.	

Case tutors from Northeastern University have devised an eight-point plan for successfully navigating online learning which is summarised below:[11]

1. Treat an online course like a 'real' course.
2. Hold yourself accountable
3. Practise time management.
4. Create a regular study space and stay organised.
5. Eliminate distractions.
6. Figure out how you learn best
7. Actively participate.
8. Leverage your network by building relationships.

8.3 RECORDING CASE DISCUSSION

It has been a long-held view that the recording of online sessions provides additional invaluable learning opportunities. Research from MIT has identified five common benefits to online learning, which can be summarised as:

1.   Enabling you to review the class afterwards.
2.   Providing greater access to case data for students with different learning styles.
3.   Enabling absent students to see what they missed.
4.   Permitting students located in different time zones to watch the session afterwards.
5.   Allowing tutors to review and monitor attendance and engagement.[12]

A word of warning: please don't see an institution's recorded case-class policy as an excuse to miss the class and simply rely on capturing the key points of the discussion through video playback. This approach totally undermines the learning potential of the case session. Not only will your peers suffer, as they do not benefit through learning from the inputs you provide to the class, but you will also suffer as you failed to get 'involved' in the *discovery* processes of learning that are at work during a case class discussion. There is an old Chinese proverb that sums up the importance of engaging with the case discission:

> Tell me and I will listen,
> Show me and I will observe,
> INVOLVE me and I will learn.

In an online case class, all students are invited to get *involved*. This is helpfully summed up by a long-established case tutor and author, John Heath who defined the case method as a

> Student discussion of a planned sequence of cases, drawn from actual situations, with responsibility for analysis and conclusions about issues within the case resting with the students. The focus is on student learning through their own joint efforts.[13]

8.4 IN SUMMARY

The Case Centre provides a wealth of resources when looking to learn with online cases.[14] By means of a conclusion, many of what might be called the *hygiene factors* for effective online case participation are aptly captured by research from Columbia Business School, which segments the essentials for effective online synchronous learning into three categories which are abridged and summarised below:[15]

1.   Clarity from your tutor
     a.   Establish clear rules of online engagement
     b.   Be clear about the precise case class instructions
     c.   Test the set-up beforehand to ensure you have access
     d.   Create a checklist for yourself
     e.   Lookout for tutor feedback
2.   Engagement
     a.   Be prepared to provide examples when called upon
     b.   Tutors might cold-call student participants

    c. Make sure you capture the feedback from polls

    d. Listen carefully to the style of questions asked

3. Accountability

    a. Your tutor should set clear expectations beforehand

    b. If you receive regular *nudges* from your tutor, it may mean you should be engaging more

    c. Be clear about how your contribution is being graded

    d. If involved in peer assessment, ensure the criteria for assessment is clear in advance

    e. Go back through the recording and note the chat conversations to draw down content, being mindful that your tutors might also be doing the same to note your contribution for grading/attendance purposes.

NOTES

1 Schiano and Andersen, 2017, p2.

2 See blog at www.northeastern.edu/graduate/blog/tips-for-taking-online-classes/

3 Pappas, 2019.

4 Schiano and Andersen, 2017, p1.

5 Muilenburg and Berge, 2005.

6 Kupp and Mueller, 2020.

7 Ayelet Israeli quoted in https://hbsp.harvard.edu/inspiring-minds/how-to-encourage-students-to-speak-up-in-virtual-classes

8 Sklar, 2020.

9 Ivey Publishing, 2020.

10 Bixler et al., 2021.

11 For further details see www.northeastern.edu/graduate/blog/tips-for-taking-online-classes/

12 Liu, Socrate and Pacheco, 2020.

13 Heath, 2015, p9.

14 For example, see www.thecasecentre.org/caseLearning/guidance/onlineCaseLearning

15 Lee, 2020.

CHAPTER 9

Remote Distance Learning with Cases

There are occasions when cases need to be delivered asynchronously, where you and your fellow students will be invited to respond to the case remotely, and not necessarily at the same time but rather over a predetermined period of time. This can prove particularly valuable when working remotely in distance-learning contexts with different learners located across continents or in different time zones, as this enables all participants to contribute at their own pace. This chapter explores differences of approach that you might adopt when participating in distance-learning, asynchronous case study sessions, and then explores the ways in which both synchronous and asynchronous learning can complement one another.

> In the asynchronous format, in which an individual case discussion can take a week, you will need a different understanding of timing.
>
> (Bentley University, US, and the Norwegian Business School[1])

> Some have claimed that the asynchronicity of asynchronous learning networks, which means that there is no pressure for an immediate response, allows for more reflection.
>
> (Open University, UK[2])

> Metacognition… has a great potential benefit for those involved in the asynchronous classroom; it focuses on one's awareness of one's own thought processes and steps taken to come to the current conclusions [and] focuses on the ability of a person to see the learning that is occurring, create a proper evaluation of the learning occurring, and then make changes in the way that they are interacting with the materials so that they can increase their overall learning.
>
> (University of Arizona, US[3])

9.1 WHAT IS AN ASYNCHRONOUS CASE SESSION?

An asynchronous case session takes place over a predetermined and prolonged period of time, where you and other participants are required to provide certain responses to questions or exercises, set by the tutor, and to provide these responses within pre-agreed time periods, while rarely requiring all students to need to log-in and contribute

DOI: 10.4324/9781003345978-12

at the same time. Progress through the case is therefore slower and more thoughtful and you can engage with the questions or exercises in your own time and at your own preferred pace. While this may seem like a less pressured environment for learning it does permit the opportunity for students to be challenged to delve deeper into key themes raised in the case than you might be expected to do in a synchronous (real-time) class discussion.

In addition to the case material and the pre-set questions or exercises, the case tutor may choose to supplement the resources for an asynchronous class with the uploading of pre-recorded video narratives to support a sense of communal engagement and personal support in what might otherwise feel like a somewhat empty environment. This presence of the tutor will no doubt bring a closer sense of reality to your class community, encouraging you in the development of a collaborative learner network or community, while often tailoring their video responses to your specific progress with the case data.

Asynchronous learning tends to rely more on peer-to-peer engagement, with *prompts* being sent to you in the early stage of the case journey, sometimes sending specific invites, and encouraging you to send answers into the online text-chat (the forum or discussion board often located onscreen to the side of the participants), so that other participants can see your comments and respond. As with synchronous case classes, the recording of all comments can then be captured by the whole group from which conclusions can be drawn and lessons (*key takeaways*) can be learnt.

9.2 BENEFITS OF ASYNCHRONOUS CASE PARTICIPATION

Perhaps not surprisingly, asynchronous case teaching often aligns well when delivering online programmes to international groups. One of the core advantages of this approach is that students have more time to formulate their response to questions, which can be particularly helpful for those students who are attempting to complete an online programme in a language that is not their mother tongue and, as such, the benefit of being permitted longer to formulate a response to the case question ensures they are better placed to overcome any language barriers. It also enables you, as the learner and case researcher, to invest more time delving deeper into the issues raised by the case, as "you can reread the case, do research, consult colleagues, and even sleep on it before taking action in the discussion."[4]

It also alleviates any stigma attached to not feeling confident enough to contribute to a normal classroom environment. Cold-calling students is almost impossible in asynchronous delivery, but tutors may occasionally nominate you with 'prompts' to provide comments or feedback on specific points, but these 'warm-calls' normally provide the learner with more time to consider a response before committing to any comment.

Carefully scheduled small group work is of even greater importance for asynchronous delivery, as is the slow release of case content to facilitate the opportunity for discovery by enhancing the expository nature of the case (in other words, you may often find that the end is not clear from the beginning). In addition to monitoring content in the text chat, you may be encouraged to journal your experiences as a reflective exercise, which would enable your tutors to tailor customised responses to your learning process on a 1:1 basis, while monitoring your engagement and performance. These responses might even contribute to some form of formative assessment or to a final summative assessment.

Multi-media cases are more popular in asynchronous contexts as any complexity associated with navigating through the digital processes of the case are offset by the opportunity to take longer to work on the problem, rather than be timebound by a synchronous class schedule.

Polling is a common activity in asynchronous case delivery (as it is in synchronous delivery) but in this case you normally have more opportunity to reflect first before committing a response. Research exploring online asynchronous case learning methods conducted by IE Business School identifies effective learning that is impacted by extensive use of discussion forums integrated with videos, simulations and online exercises.[5]

9.3 THE CASE FOR ASYNCHRONOUS LEARNING

For more than 20 years there has been a growth in literature citing research that has explored the merits of asynchronous learning, as well as highlighting many of the challenges and pitfalls. Often such citations draw attention to the importance of online learner networks. If the student community is to agree to operate in a collaborative and integrative manner then this requires an investment of time and resources to build those relationships, often despite the distance and cultural differences. The use of synchronous connection points (for example as part of an initial programme induction) can provide valuable opportunities for remote relationship-building from which you will be more naturally inclined to form bonds of trust and a willingness for collaboration with others.

> There is an inherent trade-off in the use of asynchronous group support systems for the components of a task. On the one hand, group members can reflect longer about their contributions, can participate when (and where) they choose to, can focus on those parts of the task that they like and can exchange more information. On the other hand, there are coordination problems and delayed participation may frustrate some team members, affecting the group outcomes.[6]

The importance of the social dimension to effective learning networks is explored by the Open University, UK, who undertook an ethnographic study of one of their *teaching and learning online* courses. It was discovered that the manner with which you choose to relate to your peers within an asynchronous learning community (or network) will impact the overall effectiveness of the educational experience. Positive social interactions invariably lead to a more collaborative learning environment and, not surprisingly, research endorses the view that collaborative learning is central to feelings of success and failure among students on asynchronous courses:

> Those who fell away or felt that they had failed to learn as much as they might were those who felt that they had remained outsiders unable to cross the threshold to insider status. The findings of the study point to several factors which can influence the movement of students from being outsiders to becoming insiders, including... the interaction styles of course participants.[7]

9.4 ASYNCHRONOUS *OR* SYNCHRONOUS?

Exploratory research from Canada compared both student preferences and the merits of using cases synchronously and asynchronously for online learning. This research found that there were broad differences of opinion among the same student groups, with 43% of student respondents preferring synchronous conversations and 57% preferring asynchronous discussion, but when all students were placed under examination conditions, those preferring synchronous learning correctly answered fewer items than those preferring asynchronous discussion.[8] While this research was exploratory and involved a relatively small number of students within the sample group, it nonetheless draws attention to the importance of managing your own engagement in your online case sessions whether these are synchronous, asynchronous or a combination of both.

Regardless of which approach is preferred by students, I noted one poster on a University Virtual Learning Environment (VLE) during the Covid pandemic, where students were being guided about how to manage both asynchronous and synchronous online etiquette and the following points were raised:

✓ Be Present
✓ Be Professional
✓ Be Respectful
✓ Be Aware
✓ Be Mindful
✓ Be Forgiving

9.5 ASYNCHRONOUS *AND* SYNCHRONOUS

Synchronous cases tend to work best when case material is limited in size and scope, however it is feasible to consider how some case content could be made available through asynchronous access. In this way, synchronous and asynchronous case delivery can occur independently or as a complementary and parallel approach to online learning. As Schiano and Andersen explain:

> Spending time lecturing synchronously in an online course is wasteful. If you have lecture material you feel is best delivered that way, then record the lecture, post it online, require the students to watch it, and spend the synchronous meetings fostering interaction.[9]

There is an argument that proposes that while synchronous case delivery may be a preferred approach for student exchange and shared experiential learning that supports the overall development of a learning community, by contrast asynchronous learning might provide a better approach to undertaking student assessment as well as opportunities for students to either go and explore other content to bring back to the case forum or make use of longer periods of time for case reflection and evaluation. To this end it could be argued that there are merits for your tutors deploying both synchronous and asynchronous activities simultaneously in any given online programme.

As there appears to be a growing drive towards hybrid learning programmes (incorporating both online and face-to-face approaches), as well as hyflex opportunities (where both approaches coexist simultaneously with some students engaging remotely through livestreaming while other students participate in the classroom),[10] it is likely you will discover the emergence of many more programmes where the lines between synchronous and asynchronous delivery become increasingly blurred. This is already the case in some online programmes that also incorporate occasional day-schools and weekend residentials.

> The students learned using textbooks, e-books, and videos and solved the problems independently. Then, they discussed the solutions online in groups through their WhatsApp group (asynchronously). The problem solutions were presented by the students using a class on WhatsApp or video conference platforms (synchronous).
>
> (Palangka Raya University, Indonesia[11])

9.6 IN SUMMARY

The table below lists many of the similarities and difference of approach undertaken when delivering case sessions through synchronous and asynchronous online activity:[12]

Synchronous	Asynchronous
Tutor considers pace of discussion	Students work at own pace
Fixed scheduling	Students work at a time to suit themselves
Cold call participants	Warm call participants
Tutor allows more breaks, to mitigate against online fatigue	Students choose when to engage with the case, within predetermined parameters
Tutor encourages greater use of text-chat box/discussion forum	Schedule greater use of text-chat box/discussion forum, with prompts to individuals to invite responses
Tutor makes frequent use of breakout groups	Carefully scheduled small groups
Sessions recorded for later playback and review	Tutor prepares pre-planned recorded material, time-released for students to view
Tutor draws from students in examples	Students encouraged to journal their experiences

Synchronous	Asynchronous
Expect less coverage in the discussion time than face-to-face sessions	Similar coverage over a longer period of reflective time
Screen sharing encouraged	Often slower/phased release of case content
Utilise lots of polls	Utilise lots of polls

NOTES

1 Schiano and Andersen, 2017, p2.
2 Wegerif, 2019, p43.
3 Varkey et al., 2023, p9.
4 Schiano and Andersen, 2017, p9.
5 Gabaldón, 2020.
6 Benbaum-Fich, Hiltz and Turoff, 2001, p461; see also Morse, 2003; and Valenta et al., 2001.
7 Wegerif, 2019, p48.
8 Johnson and Buck, 2007.
9 Schiano and Andersen, 2017, p6.
10 Kyei-Blankson et al., 2014.
11 Mairing et al., 2021, p190.
12 Andrews, 2021.

SECTION C

Using Cases for My Assessments

So far, we have looked at how to learn using case studies that are based on class discussions – both face-to-face and online. This next section looks at how to plan for developing assignments involving case studies. It makes sense that if your tutor is using case studies in class as a regular tool for learning, then your assessments should be related to the case studies in some form. This section is segmented into two chapters, the first of which looks at how you might prepare for case assignments and examinations and considers a range of different types of expectations and responses demanded by a case assessment brief. The second chapter explores how you might go about developing our own case study where this is a set-piece requirement for a module assignment. Once again, examples from real practitioners from different business locations around the world have been used to inform these chapters.

DOI: 10.4324/9781003345978-13

CHAPTER 10

How Do I Use Cases in Assignments and Exams?

If you are using cases regularly in your programme, then it is likely that some of your assignments are going to use cases too. Often you will be able to preview your case prior to the assignment or exam but sometimes you may be required to evaluate a case 'blindly' with no prior insights into the organisation or situation under review. This chapter explores key approaches to preparing to work with cases in an assignment or examination context, providing a checklist of potential questions to explore as part of your preparations.

> Sometimes case reports are used in conjunction with case discussion or even presentation. In the first instance, they may be handed in before or after class and are often used to test the quality of student preparation.... In the second instance, they may be required by the instructor to accompany a presentation for evaluation purposes.
>
> (Richard Ivey School of Business, Canada[1])

This is one of many examples of the types of approaches adopted by case tutors when setting assignments associated with case discussions. There are many different approaches adopted by case tutors when planning assessments for case-based programmes, but most tend to ensure you are applying the same types of analytical 'case-detective' skills that we have explored in previous chapters (especially the seven principal considerations explored in Chapter 2).

10.1 ASSESSING IN-CLASS CASE DISCUSSIONS

If you know that the case method will form part of your module assessment, then it is important to gain a clear understanding of what exactly is being assessed. In some circumstances, tutors may be assessing your actual verbal contribution in a case class discussion. This might include any presentations you are asked to make as individuals or in groups. If in-class contribution is being assessed, then there are a number of approaches that might be worth considering.

There might be a tendency to think that just saying something must be better than nothing, but the peril here is that a poorly considered response could work against you as

DOI: 10.4324/9781003345978-14

much as a general reluctance to contribute to a discussion. Things to avoid when discussing might include:

- simply restating what has already been stated in the case, without any form of analysis or interpretation;
- repeating something that a previous student mentioned;
- making generalised statements that don't really contribute anything new to the discussion;
- becoming over-verbose – using ten sentences to state what could have been more succinctly stated in one sentence;
- over-analysis of a situation with unlikely or unrealistic predictions;
- comments that are not related to the specific area under discussion at that point in time.

By contrast, contributions to a class discussion that are likely to be rewarded might include:

- a discussion starter – a willingness to break the ice when no one else is willing to start a discussion;
- providing new, fresh, and insightful comments;
- being clear and persuasive in your discussion;
- demonstrating mental agility and a balanced perspective of the situation under review;
- demonstrating a clear response based on sound analysis;
- adopting a respectful humility towards other contributors

Most module assessments would normally include a briefing document, and these often contain a grading matrix. A review of this grading matrix is essential as it will help you to gain a better understanding of what the case tutor is looking to test with this case assessment. For example, some assessments may be mostly focused on your capacity to demonstrate a deeper level of understanding of your specific *subject discipline*, to apply known theory in a relevant manner, or to compare and contrast your analysis of a particular situation to other known situations of a similar nature that may have been discussed previously in class, or that may have been recently profiled in the business press. By contrast, other case assessments may be more focused on testing the *management skills* that you have developed during previous case sessions and to see how these are demonstrated under test conditions. Some of these were highlighted in Chapter 2 and include:

- Analysis and critical thinking
- Decision-making
- Judging between courses of action
- Handling assumptions and inferences
- Presenting different points of view
- Listening to and understanding others

10.2 USING CASES IN WRITTEN ASSESSMENTS

If you are required to provide a written report as part of your case assessment, then be clear about the parameters of the report and stick to them. You may feel that adopting additional content that has not been asked for might provide opportunities for bonus marks, but if these 'extras' were not aligned to anything within the assessment's grading matrix then they are wasted words that could have been better allocated to the questions that you are being asked to address.

Here's a checklist of questions that you might like to consider when preparing for a case assignment:

- Is this a case you are already familiar with?
- Has it already been discussed in class?
- If so, was the class recorded and are there notes from the session that are worth reviewing again?
- What questions were asked in class and how do these inform or align with the questions raised for the assignment?
- If the case is about a known company, then are there any other resources you can access in order to find further information relevant to the case questions and to inform your response?
- What themes are made explicit and implicit within the case questions that will need a targeted response?
- How have these themes been addressed in other case discussions or similar class exercises?
- How long do you have to complete the assessment?
- How many questions are there?
- Are they all equally weighted? If not, then approximately what proportion of the wordcount should you allocate to each question?

Always map out your response before starting to complete each section of your assignment and regularly refer back to the objectives of the assessment and any other details provided in the assessment guidelines or grading matrix to ensure you are meeting all the listed criteria.

And remember the Toulmin model of argumentation (see Chapter 4). This will really help you to determine a clear critical approach when building an evidence-based, theory-informed response to any questions or issues you are required to address.

Here's a typical example of a case study assignment brief:

Assignment task(s): *This assignment requires you to submit an evidence-based critical evaluation of change leadership practice demonstrated in the ABC Ltd Case Study available on your VLE from the start of your programme.*

Assessment briefing: *This document provides details of the assessment. There will also be oral briefings conducted in weeks 4 and 11.*

Assessment criteria: *Specific criteria are listed below, and further details can be found in the Grading Matrix in Appendix A. Your 3,000-word written report should provide the following:*

- *A summary of two or three key change leadership issues/themes specifically related to the case study and evaluated against academic literature.*
- *Critical analysis of leadership approaches of the stakeholders in the case study*
- *If you were the CEO for ABC Ltd what may you have done differently, giving reasons for your view, with relevant links to the academic literature.*
- *What other suggestion(s) for future sustainable change would you propose which might enable the organisation to continue to thrive, drawing insights from current leadership research and thinking.*

An extract from a typical grading matrix related to this assignment, demonstrating the criteria and requirements for an A grade are illustrated in the table below:

Assessment Criteria

GRADE	Summary of change and leadership issues 20%	Critical analysis of leadership and change frameworks 30%	Alternative change strategies 20%	Future sustainable change 20%	Presentation of report and evidence 10%
A	Starting with a hypothesis arising from current academic debate, identifies 2–3 key change and leadership issues which are summarised objectively.	Synthesises and critically evaluates multiple theoretical frameworks with conclusions, making some contribution to the understanding of the change and leadership discipline.	An innovative solution building on the original hypothesis and critical analysis of literature, continuing to develop a personal line of argument.	Weighs up conflicting options for future change leading from the arguments in previous section. An innovative, ethical, and inclusive change solution is proposed.	High-quality written presentation referenced accurately using the Harvard Referencing criteria. Demonstrated ability to write complex and challenging ideas persuasively. Proofread and edited.

By reflecting on this case study assignment brief and the grading matrix, in light of the points raised previously in this chapter, you will acquire a number of important insights to help you as part of your preparation for this assignment. A quick glimpse at the grading matrix and it becomes immediately clear that not all elements of the assignment's requirements are equally weighted, so that enables you to consider approximately what proportion of your 3,000-word allowance you will allocate to each section.

The briefing document makes clear from the onset that the assessor is looking for an *evidence-based* approach with *critical evaluation*, focusing on *change leadership* practices that are demonstrated in an *ABC Ltd Case Study* which was made available to you on *your VLE from the start of your programme*. This assignment brief document goes on to inform you that oral briefings *are provided in weeks 4 and 11* so it will be worth reviewing any notes that were taken during these tutorial sessions and to check the VLE to see if any additional supportive/guiding documents were provided (or their links provided) during these briefing sessions.

The 'Assessment criteria' section gets to the heart of what you need to deliver in your report and provides clear explanations of what was meant by *evidence-based* and *critical evaluation*. Once again, the term *critical evaluation* should inspire you to look-up Toulmin or a similar model of argumentation. It is worth noting not only what you are being asked to produce but also what you are not being asked to produce. You are not being asked to 'describe' anything or to make up your own unwarranted suggestions, but rather all elements of the report need to be backed up by evidence and/or literature from appropriate academic sources. If Toulmin's model is applied, then you will ensure there are 'grounds' and 'backers' for all your 'claims'. 'Unwarranted claims' will not credit you with any points in your assessment. This part of the assessment brief also invites you to reflect on what is an appropriate academic source. While it may be entirely relevant to include news and trade press articles that relate to the situation/issues under review in the case assignment, the assignment brief is clear in its expectation that you should cross-reference your statements and comments to scholarly reviewed literature (most often found in academic journals). Do ensure when you are citing other references that they are credible and that within the text you are including a clear explanation of what it is that this reference has contributed to your thinking about the issue under investigation. And always ensure your approach to citations and referencing is consistent and follows the expected criteria of your institute, in this example using the Harvard Referencing model (as indicated in the grading matrix).

An appraisal of the four bullet points indicates that you are expected to produce a *summary of two or three points* (evaluated against academic literature), a *critical analysis*, provide reasoned *alternative* courses of action and *proposals for the future* (noting the comment about *sustainable change*). The first bullet point requires you to focus on *two or three issues/themes* and the A grade first column of the grading matrix indicates the grading is for an *identification of two or three change leadership issues*, which would suggest that if you were to choose four, five or six themes it is unlikely that these would achieve any additional credits. The second bullet point refers to *stakeholders*, inferring that your response should reflect more than one individual. The third bullet point invites you to step into the shoes of one of the key stakeholders (the CEO) and propose alternatives, but these should not be mere suggestions or assertions, but rather they need to be provided with clear reasoning and referencing to literature (*backers* and *qualifiers*). The last bullet point invites you to think about other examples from comparable organisations, as well as other scholarly references, to argue the adequacy of your recommendations.

Your assignment brief will no doubt provide details about how the report should be set out. If you are asked to include an *Executive Summary*, then remember this is different to an *Introduction*. Normally an Executive Summary should provide a brief summary of every section of your report, which might include the analysis, evaluation, recommendations and conclusions (where such items are requested as part of the overall report structure). Always ensure you have checked your citations against a *bibliography* at the end of the report. It is quite common practice to include a *table of contents* and to include page numbers that align with your contents page. You may also wish to include *exhibits* as *appendices* at the end of the report (unless guided against such action).

10.3 THE CASE PRESENTATION

Your tutor may include a case presentation as a part of your module assessment, which could be delivered either as an individual or as part of a group or syndicate. Presentations provide an opportunity for you to showcase your case analysis skills both visually and verbally and are a great way of ensuring every student voice is heard as part of a case exercise. If you are working as a group, it might be a requirement that only one person from the group speaks during the presentation on behalf of their peers. If this is required, then it is important to ensure there is a fair and equitable sharing of roles and responsibilities in the group's preparation for the presentation. Planning and preparation are key skills being developed as part of this exercise:

> In group presentations considerable thought must be placed on who says what and in which order. Special care should be devoted to your opening to arouse interest and get the class attention; and to your conclusion as it may provide a lasting impression.
>
> (Richard Ivey School of Business, Canada[2])

When preparing for your presentation, do ensure you have practised beforehand with a *dry run* (ideally to a live group) to test the effectiveness, persuasiveness and impact of both your verbal statements and your visuals. Time your practice run-through of the presentation to ensure you are remaining within the given scheduling criteria and if you exceed this then consider what information you might look to prune from the presentation rather than planning to speak faster to cram more in. One common weakness of presentations is to include so much data that it becomes unintelligible, and your core points get lost amid the myriad of secondary points. Always remember to *keep the main thing the plain thing.* When using slides always ensure these are readable and not unduly complex or content-heavy. Ensure there has been sufficient time allocated for every slide to ensure all the relevant data from each slide can be captured by the reader and assimilated. Avoid use of inappropriate jargon and remember this is a management case study and so it may help to adopt a mindset as if you are presenting to a management team. It may help further to test your visuals for system compatibility before being called to deliver your presentation as you don't want to find yourself with problems accessing content while people are kept waiting prior to your delivery. Always consider a back-up plan in case your content is inaccessible.

Often after a presentation, the tutor may invite questions from your audience. This can often be one of the most stressful parts of your presentation as it is the least predictable part of it. However, you can mitigate against this by anticipating what types of questions might be asked and rehearse stock responses to such questions. You might even provide hints during your presentation, with leading statements, to invite questions for which responses should have already been prepared. One thing to avoid is becoming over-defensive. This is a natural human behavioural response to a stress situation such as a Q&A session, but you will perform better if you can condition yourself to avoid defensive responses. Think about your body posture and try not to fold your arms at this stage and tie your body up in knots. Take a breath, take your time, even remind the enquirer what a good question this is (that response alone buys you an extra five seconds of thinking time), and then proceed to provide your answer. If you genuinely don't know how to respond to a question or don't understand what is being asked, then it is perfectly reasonable to ask the enquirer if they might rephrase the question as you are struggling to understand what is being requested.

Peer Assessment

Occasionally, you might be asked to assess others within your class as part of the overall grading process. Peer assessment is becoming increasingly common, even though it is fraught with objective complexities. It does, however, mirror common practice in many workplace contexts, so it is perhaps not surprising that you might be asked to participate in a peer assessment as part of a case group exercise, especially if you have been working in a group to develop a report or presentation. When being asked to undertake a peer assessment, be clear about the processes and procedures that need to underpin your response, and be honest and clear in your response, ensuring that you have considered how you might defend your statements if ever challenged to do so. A peer assessment is never your opportunity to 'get your own back' on an individual with whom you may have had a disagreement as this would wholly undermine the grading process and undoubtedly create further troubles for you later in the programme.

10.4 USING CASES IN EXAMINATIONS

If your module is to be assessed by examination and a case study is to be used in this context then there are extra layers of complexity to consider, as you are undoubtedly going to be required to tackle certain tasks under time-constrained examination conditions, which adds extra pressures to your ability to provide a full and broadly considered response.

> One of the most common failings of case exams is that writers don't offer the reader a clear cut position statement. A variant is to say that there are a number of possible positions but not commit to any. To the reader, an essay that begins this way makes the writer look evasive and afraid to take a position.
>
> (Harvard, US[3])

Case examinations can take a number of different forms and all the assessment questions listed in the previous section apply, but in addition you might also want to consider:

- Will the case study be accessible prior to the exam?
- If not, how much additional time (if any) is permitted to read and appraise the case prior to the official start of the exam?
- Will the exam questions be known prior to the exam?
- Are you permitted to bring notes with you into the exam?
- Are you allowed to access the internet to explore issues related to the company?
- What are the grading criteria for the exam (often found in a grading matrix in an examination brief)?

10.5 ONE FINAL THOUGHT – SO WHAT?

Once again it is worth asking the *so what?* question, given that the assignments in themselves may offer you some really valuable learning experiences. Increasingly these days, scholars are being encouraged to consider not just an assessment *of* learning but also assessments *for* learning; or put another way, your assessment experience ought also to be contributing to your overall learning from the programme. This might, for example, be derived from examiner/assessor feedback after the grading has been completed. If this is not immediately forthcoming, then it is within your prerogative to request that your tutor offers you some response to how you might learn lessons from your performance to make improvements for future similar exercises. And don't forget to log it (see Chapter 5). If you've been adopting a learning log for self-reflection throughout the module, then make sure you include the learning derived from your assessment experiences too.

10.6 IN SUMMARY

In summary, this chapter has:

- introduced you to different approaches to undertaking case study-related assessments including both verbal and written assessment;
- provided a checklist of the types of questions you might want to ask prior to beginning your assessment;
- considered the types of processes and procedures for assessment and explored what exactly is the focus of an individual or group assessment.

NOTES

1 Mauffette-Leenders, Erskine and Leenders, 2007, p107.
2 Ibid., p105.
3 Ellet, 2018, p115.

CHAPTER 11

How Do I Construct My Own Case for a Class Assignment?

Drafting your own case study based on your evaluations of an organisation is a common assignment approach adopted by case tutors. Normally you will be provided with a prescription to adopt which identifies the boundaries and parameters for your research. This chapter takes you through commonly deployed approaches to developing a case for a class assignment. It also addresses the implications for working in a group context to develop the case.

> I usually specify that the organisation chosen must be at least one year old and must employ a number of people so that the roles and functions covered in the coursework are represented. Students should look at organisations with easily accessible information so that they can quickly assess whether or not an analysis will be possible.
>
> (New Zealand[1])

While there are various ways of assessing your own, personally drafted case study, it is quite common for you to be asked to 'present or deliver' your case as some form of individual or group presentation once the case construction process has been completed. This participative approach unavoidably gets you more engaged with the case method as it often invites you to consider the *discovery* element of the learning process.

To enable this approach to be effective you will benefit from having personally experienced case delivery in class beforehand and you will need some careful guidance on case writing approaches to ensure you are able to facilitate a journey of discovery for both yourself and your audience. I've often found that when I introduce this assessment approach with students, it also motivates them to be more engaged as participants in future case class discussions, as they have a greater appreciation for the learning process.

11.1 A TYPICAL CASE STUDY TEMPLATE

Often a template for the class is prepared and distributed as part of the assignment brief, which you should then use to form the basis for your case planning, alongside a copy of a 'mapping' template which you might use to help guide and steer the case development process and to avoid it becoming excessively onerous. A typical prescription for a case assignment of this nature might include:

DOI: 10.4324/9781003345978-15

1.   Title – related to the company
2.   Subtitle – related to the theme/subject matter
3.   Opening paragraph – which identifies the problem
4.   Second paragraph – that introduces the context/situation and the organisation
5.   Third paragraph – identifies the key characters in the case
6.   Core body of text: No more than three pages
7.   Conclusion – reinforcing the main focus of the case
8.   References
9.   Exhibits, tables or diagrams – no more than four

I normally stipulate that an accompanying 'map' should include at least one (and no more than three) aspects of management theory that might be explored or applied in relation to your case data. In my case-writing and presentation assignments, students are then given 30 minutes to facilitate a short 'journey' through their case data.

11.2 THE CASE MAP

Figure 11.1 provides a template for a map that my students might be invited to construct to accompany their case study.

Given the level of investment that I ensure my students have made to deliver their short case sessions, I check to make certain that each session receives feedback, not only

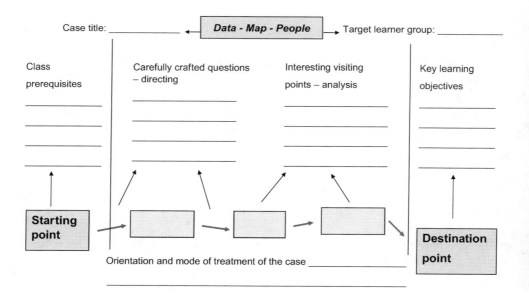

FIGURE 11.1 Case Study Mapping Template

on the appropriateness of subject matter and level of depth of the case content, but also on the manner with which it was facilitated in the class session. I am keen to point out the positive communication and people skills that were evident and draw attention to how important these will be for future employability. If you find this is not already forthcoming, then I would encourage you to seek feedback afterwards to ensure that your reflections (and those of your tutor and peers) are contributing to your overall learning from this exercise.

Research from Richard Ivey School of Business, Canada draw attention to the positive reasons why such student-researched, student-facilitated case presentations can be an effective way to support your learning. They cite a range of purposes which are summarised below:[2]

- Adds variety to the learning experience
- Develops presentation skills
- Develops communication skills
- Experiences in line with making briefings to senior management
- Emphasises action and implementation planning
- Develops prioritising skills
- Develops time management skills
- Practice in using audio and visual supports
- Forces participants to prepare
- Develops practice in managing group dynamics
- Promotes active listening and evaluation skills

11.3 DEVELOPING YOUR CASE STUDY AS PART OF A GROUP EXERCISE

If you are being asked to develop a case study as part of a small group, then it is important to establish from the onset how the roles of group members are to be shared. This ensures you are as efficient and impactful as possible within the timeframe set for the assignment.

Here are a few case writing hints to help promote clarity during your case writing process:

- Keep the case writer(s) out of the case, unless the case is specifically about you or one of your team.
- When collating data from key stakeholders or protagonists in a case study, their opinions may be more important than the case facts.
- As you write the case, check all the verbs and adjectives for the impression they convey.
- Consider your choice of words and sentence length to ensure the words are appropriate for your target audience and that sentence length promotes greater readability.
- Explore changing the pace of the narrative from time to time as this can enhance engagement with the case data.

- Consider using quotations as this can bring your case study alive and support that aspiration of creating a slice of reality.
- Watch out to ensure you are not guilty of repetition, especially if more than one person has contributed to the final version of the case.
- Consider different means of representing data.
- Check the internal consistency and overall emphasis of the case.

Once you have all completed your individual work collating data to inform each section of your case study, ensure one person from within your group has been agreed to provide final editorial control. Failure to do this might lead to a very misshapen final version of your case study – more akin to an *indigestible case sandwich*, as each contributor provides a slightly different approach or writing style to their section of the case. This approach will undoubtedly undermine the final overall readability of the case.

Most importantly, if you have used primary data that you have derived from an organisation as part of your case research, then you must ensure you have some form of written *formal release authorisation* from the company to permit you to use the data as part of your case study. This is an important safeguarding function to avoid potential legal action being taken should another representative from the same organisation deem the data to be unsuitable for your use or for wider external circulation.

If you or your case writing group are being asked to subsequently present your written case in class, then here is a short checklist of a few things you may wish to consider:

- What questions does your case address and how will these be raised in your presentation?
- What approach will you adopt with your allotted presentation time – for example, a formal presentation, a classroom discussion, or some form of role play?
- How will you open the case presentation?
- What are the key themes within your presentation and how will discussion flow from one theme to the next, ensuring that any debating points are also included?
- How will data be presented and reviewed during the case presentation?
- What other exercises might you adopt during the presentation to engage all the viewers?
- What approach will you adopt to close any discussion, capture key learning points, and draw your presentation to a conclusion?
- What visuals will you use and who will be responsible for these while you are delivering the case? (Managing group dynamics and mobilising all members of the project group.)

11.4 AND FINALLY

Occasionally, I have found that when a tutor adopts a case-writing assessment such as those listed above then sometimes the quality of the final case is so good that it deserves to be used more widely for case teaching in the future, and tutors have found themselves working with the student after the completion of the course assignment to adapt their case for future teaching purposes. So, you never know, your case-writing assessment could be the first step towards publishing new case teaching material that might be adopted in other business schools in the future to promote learning to a much wider audience.

11.5 IN SUMMARY

In summary, this chapter has:

- introduced you to different approaches to writing a case study for a class assignment;
- provided a checklist of the different elements of a case;
- explored using a case map to plot your journey through the case data to promote opportunities for learning as part of a group discussion.

NOTES

1   Van der Ham, 2016, p14.
2   Erskine, Leenders and Mauffette-Leenders, 2003.

SECTION D

Using Cases for My Research

The first three sections of this book explored how we use the case method as a tool for learning and assessment, both in the classroom and online, and this section explores how the case method has evolved as a technique for conducting qualitative research.

If you are conducting research as part of your studies, you will no doubt have started to think about the different types of approaches that you can adopt to undertake research and design research projects.

Most good research methods textbooks will encourage you to think very carefully about the overall research process before determining the most suitable approach for the type of research that you wish to undertake.

This section begins with Chapter 12, which explores the types of approaches to the case method that you might employ for your qualitative research project. Then Chapter 13 examines approaches to gathering data to inform case development and Chapter 14 considers how you might then explore analysing the data from your case(s) to address your research objectives.

DOI: 10.4324/9781003345978-16

What Types of Qualitative Case Research Approach Should I Adopt?

This chapter focuses on using a case study approach as a methodology for undertaking qualitative research. This is a commonly utilised method, particularly for dissertation modules at both undergraduate and postgraduate levels, for which there are a range of different approaches that might be adopted. This chapter provides a set of terms to help explain the use of the case method as a research strategy, evaluates the contexts and likely opportunities that best lend themselves to a case-based approach, and examines the different models and techniques that can be deployed.

The case method is one of a number of techniques or strategies that you might wish to explore if your project is located in qualitative research. But its use in research has been interpreted in many different ways by scholars and there are numerous ideas about how to adopt the case method in research. This section will look at what other scholars have had to say about this and try to demystify the case method as a research strategy.

Most scholars agree that the case method in research is normally seen as a research strategy that can be applied in qualitative research – or, as Denzin and Lincoln describe it: "a situated activity that locates the observer in the world," and likely consists of "a set of interpretive, material practises that make the world visible."[1]

Let's start from the beginning: qualitative research, in contrast to quantitative research, normally involves the study, analysis and appraisal of observational data that can be received through processes of interpretive inquiry using techniques such as interviews, focus groups, personal experience and case studies. These types of processes enable you, as the researcher, to "explore the *how* and *why* questions about real-life events, using a broad variety of empirical tools."[2]

One very useful diagrammatic approach to understanding research methods is provided by Saunders, Lewis and Thornhill in their book *Research Methods for Business Students*,[3] which presents what has commonly been referred to as the 'research onion' method to determining your preferred research approach. As you can see from Figure 12.1, each section or layer of their 'onion' diagram enables you, as the researcher, to design the various stages of your research process to determine the approach most appropriate for your specific project. You are invited to effectively peel back the layers (as you might do with an onion) to arrive at your determined research approach. This process of working through the onion begins with determining your *research philosophy*, then to consider different *approaches for theory development* before determining your *methodological choice*.

DOI: 10.4324/9781003345978-17

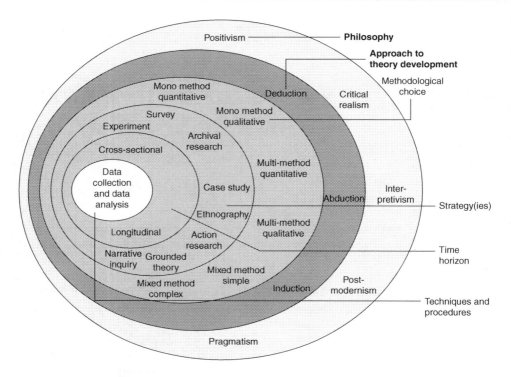

FIGURE 12.1 Research Onion

Source: M. N. K. Saunders, P. Lewis and A. Thornhill (2019), *Research Methods for Business Students* (Eighth Edition) Harlow: Pearson, p 130. The research onion diagram is ©2018 Mark Saunders, Philip Lewis and Adrian Thornhill and is reproduced in this book with their written permission.

From this point your *strategy* can be developed and various *techniques and procedures* can be selected depending on the *time horizon* of your research. On the basis of this framework, the case method is a commonly adopted *strategy* which can be deployed using a variety of *techniques* (such as single case or multiple case) when adopting an *interpretive philosophy*, applying a *deductive* approach as part of a single or multi-method qualitative research *methodology*.

As soon as you open your research textbooks, you'll find that perceptions of research methods are constantly evolving and opinions are frequently changing about the relevance and the recommended types of research methods that you might adopt. Some approaches to undertaking research have a long tried-and-tested history, while others are considered to be more contemporary, and some critics have long-argued about the appropriateness of certain practices.

So, when using the case method as your chosen approach to your project it is important for you to have a really clear rationale for your choice, in case you are called upon to argue the adequacy of your selected approach in the future. To get you started, some initial questions you might wish to ask are:

• What is the purpose of my research?
• What resources do I have available to me to support me in my research?

- What types of questions am I looking to address?
- What timescales do I have to work within?

Developing case studies has become a very popular phenomena and one that is not simply reserved for teaching purposes or for scholarly research. The term is widely used in businesses looking to showcase good practice or in newspaper articles, online blogs or news items positioned to explore a particular real-life incident or situation, whether that is located with an individual, organisation, programme, group of people, institution or a specific event. In fact, most business and social science textbooks on most subject matters tend to incorporate what they refer to as case studies to demonstrate or apply a particular point or theme that has been the focus of that particular chapter. So, the case study has evolved as a commonplace literary term, whereas if you were to step back a few years – as recently as the 1980s – you would find that the case study as an academic qualitative research approach was a less frequently considered option and a commonly misunderstood research strategy, the meaning and value of which led to some highly critical reviews from some scholars. So, it is perhaps not surprising that the adoption of the case method in qualitative research requires clear positioning within research literature and a more precise explanation of the specific methodologies that you are looking to adopt to ensure you are confident that you can clearly justify your approach. Nowadays case study research has emerged as one of the five most accepted forms of qualitative research, alongside narrative research, phenomenology, grounded theory and ethnography.[4]

12.1 DIVERGENT VIEWS ON WHAT IS A CASE

In the early period of conceptualising around the case method as a research strategy, three scholars: Yin, Bryman and Stake are recognised as most frequently cited, and subsequently long-established, contributors to discussions on the evolving acceptance of the case method as a credible strategy for qualitative research.[5]

> In general, case studies are the preferred strategy when "how" or "why" questions are being posed, when the investigator has little or no control over events, and when the focus is on a contemporary phenomenon within some real-life context… Where the case study allows an investigation to retain the holistic and meaningful characteristics of real-life events such as individual life-cycles, organisational and managerial processes.[6]

Views differ on what exactly a case study is in the context of scholarly research, so it is helpful to explore what scholars have had to say about the case method before we get started on selecting your preferred technique. For example, Bryman[7] claims that the case study is a *strategy* that normally enables you, the researcher, to capture the case participant's perceptions of real-life experiences, as well as revealing their values, better than comparable studies which employ surveys or other experimental strategies. Saunders, Lewis and Thornhill also affirm the 'case study' as a research *strategy*, whereas Stake argues that a case study is not a methodological choice but rather a choice of 'object' to be studied. Bryman affirms this view that the case is an object of interest in its own right and suggests that the role of the researcher is to provide an in-depth elucidation of it and in particular to identify and focus on the unique features of the case – a process referred to as the idiographic approach.

Schwandt and Gates propose that there is no single understanding of a case study, but that the ways that each are

> defined and employed varies considerably across disciplines and fields of study including sociology, anthropology, political science, organisational research, history, psychology, clinical medicine and therapeutic practice, educational research, policy analysis and program evaluation.[8]

They extend the boundaries of case study research to include both qualitative and quantitative methods.

Ragin and Becker take a slightly broader perspective by presenting a map for understanding what a case is, within which it can either be understood as an empirical unit where the 'case' is already available and discoverable (i.e., to be found); or as a theoretical construct where the case is to be made,[9] and they argue that cases can be viewed either as configurations or as a combination of characteristics.

In summary, the case study strategy that works best for you will be determined by the types of 'how' and 'why' research questions you are seeking to address, the number of cases you are looking to use, the role and purpose of the case, and the degree to which it is to be used in isolation or to complement a broader research strategy. Mixed method research strategies might, for example, deploy a case study methodology alongside a more quantitative approach using other data for statistical analysis. Used together, these types of strategies often ensure broader generalisations can be justified while identifying examples and insights from cases for analytical generalisation.

12.2 HOW MANY CASE STUDIES SHOULD I USE IN MY RESEARCH PROJECT?

Yin is one of the most widely quoted scholars on the use of the case study method in research and he proposes that there are various forms of case study research that might include a single case based on one individual or organisation, or that case study research might involve the use of multiple cases based on more than one individual, organisation or context. Flyvbjerg argues against previously held views that you cannot generalise from an individual case and that it should not be adopted as a strategy for a theory-building (inductive) approach to research. Denzin and Lincoln support this argument suggesting that, while it might not always be the most desirable approach, you can generalise from an individual case as has historically been attributed to practices associated with Darwin, Newton and Einstein.[10] So it is reasonable to conclude that there are a range of views related to how a case study approach for research should be constructed and, once again, perhaps the most important takeaway for you to note from this is to ensure that you have clearly argued the adequacy of the choices that you make when determining your own research approach.

Yin proposes that both single and multiple case study strategies can be adopted within a similar methodological framework and suggests that there might also be either single or multiple units of analysis adopted within the strategy design. Gerring, for example, argues for a single point of analysis suggesting that a case study should be

> an intensive study of a single unit... a spatially bounded phenomenon – e.g. a nation-state, revolution, political party, election, or person – observed at a single point in time or over some delimited period of time.[11]

By contrast, if you are intending to work with a single and yet complex case approach then your case might include inputs from a wide range of informants from different departments or contexts from within the case organisation, to enable you to capture a richer picture, that could include attitudes or behaviours which have been informed by experiences, opinions and reactions. Patton asserts that capturing multiple perspectives within a single case forms essential components of social constructionist research.[12] However, there are arguably limitations to the degree to which a single case study can enable broader generalisations. Stake argues that the object of a social enquiry is seldom an individual enterprise and as such one single case study in isolation "is seen to be a poor basis for generalisation."[13] By contrast, when unique features are expressed in different ways in a number of different organisations or 'cases' then different observations can be made by comparing one case with another in what is referred to as a *cross-sectional design*. Yin asserts that not surprisingly the adoption of a multiple case approach might have distinct advantages compared to single cases when it comes to arguing the adequacy of the evidence drawn from its analysis, and in most scenarios the multiple case approach would be regarded as more robust. However, this depends on the purpose of the case and how unusual, novel, unique or revelatory the case might appear. This view is supported by Willis who argues that the scope for single case study analysis is limited by "the inter-related issues of methodological rigour, researcher subjectivity, and external validity."[14]

Cross-sectional cases adopt a nomothetic research approach in that they explore statements (or habits) that apply regardless of time and place. Bryman argues that when qualitative research is employed within a cross-sectional design, then the approach tends to be inductive, in terms of the relationship between theory and research (i.e., it is theory-generating).[15]

There is however, no hard or fast rule when determining how many cases should be included in your case research strategy and while there is evidence of plenty of projects supporting the use of just a single case, there are as many that support the idea of drawing insights from a multiple case study approach. Some scholars argue that the multi-case approach to research works best when it is developed from a rich theoretical framework (i.e., deductive) and that, as such, an initial trial of one or two cases can be used to further inform a theoretical basis by acting as a feedback loop for an ongoing, iterative study which could result in an overall conceptual approach, which can therefore be considered both inductive and deductive.[16]

Whichever strategy you choose to adopt it is worth considering that the goal for the case method, as May asserts, is "to overcome dichotomies between generalizing and particularizing, quantitative and qualitative, deductive and inductive techniques."[17]

12.3 SELECTING THE RIGHT CASE TECHNIQUE FOR YOUR PROJECT

Determining the right technique for a case strategy is part of what Yin refers to as the research design process. This process involves "a logical plan for getting from here to there where here may be defined as the set of questions to be addressed, and there is some set of conclusions about these questions."[18] Unavoidably your research questions will play a key role in determining the options available to you in designing a process that best enables you to draw meaningful conclusions. Gomm, Hammersley and Foster examine four methodological issues when addressing the purpose and nature of the case study strategy:

- Its generalisability
- Causal or narrative analysis
- The nature of theory
- Authenticity and authority[19]

In the first instance they ask how the case technique can be best devised to provide an acceptable opportunity for *generalisations*. Such generalisations need to be able to draw from sufficient evidence to provide credibility to the conclusions that are drawn, without resorting to an evidence-based approach that is built upon inferences which are drawn, for example, from statistical analysis. Statistical analysis might well enable empirical generalisations whereas case studies provide what Yin refers to as *analytical* generalisations.[20] In some situations, scholars have argued that case strategies can provide some level of generalisation, even when only based on one case, while others have taken this approach further to examine the potential transferability of findings from one context to another. Clearly, the breadth and depth of data that is drawn upon to develop the case will impact its perceived capacity to provide a natural basis for generalisation.

In contrast to such generalisations, Bennett and Elman identify an alternative advantage of a single case study strategy where the case is implicitly *comparative* or what might be referred to as a *deviant case*, which would include those for which such an outcome would not fit with previously determined theoretical expectations or with commonly accepted empirical patterns.[21]

Where cases have been able to capture data derived over a significant period of time, their subsequent analysis might permit conclusions that identify *causal processes*; a technique that Brady and Collier refer to as causal-process observation.[22] In contrast, some might suggest that research typically involves creating an artificial (controlled) environment within which to undertake certain experiments, and from which to identify potential causal processes. But it is argued that this artificial approach often fails to examine the causal process in the context of real-world situations. The narrative style of a written case study, unpacking a historical sequence of events, provides such opportunities to explore causal processes, or put another way you, as the researcher, can see the causal processes. But for this to work effectively your choice of cases is vital and the breadth and depth to which your narrative (reporting) style captures comparative content is also a key factor:

> The most powerful version of comparative measure is experimentation, which involves creating the cases that are required for testing a causal claim. By contrast, the case study researcher has to search for naturally occurring cases that will provide the necessary comparative leverage.[23]

Blatter and Blume propose that identifying causal processes is one of three distinct approaches to using case studies in research – the other two approaches being co-variational (or comparative) case research and congruence analysis. Most scholars agree that the use of cases for co-variational (comparative) research is the most popular approach, and this will be discussed further in Chapter 14, but the use of cases for congruence analysis is also growing in popularity as it is strongly *theory-centred*. Blatter and Blume argue that a co-variational approach "is aiming to draw generalizing conclusions from cases to a wider population, whereas causal process tracing strives to get deeper and denser insights, and congruence analysis is used in order to address a broader theoretical discourse."[24]

Congruence analysis is defined by Blatter and Blume as an approach that focuses on drawing inferences from the (non-)congruence of concrete observations with specified predictions from abstract theories. They go on to explore the use (relevance/relative strength) of theories to help explain or make sense of the case(s), by observing matches between empirical findings and concrete expectations that are deduced from core elements of theories. This requires the researcher to purposively reflect on the relationship between such theories and the observations that were made from the case(s). Theories can be applied or further developed using this approach, and hence both a deductive and/or inductive approach can be adopted.

Gomm, Hammersley and Foster's fourth methodological issue refers to the *authenticity and authority* of drawing conclusions using the case method. This can be addressed through a number of questions. For example, as you are developing your case(s), how can you demonstrate its authenticity? To what degree have the techniques you have employed ensured that the case is as unbiased and as true a reflection of life as it can be? This might typically be addressed by considering the agents or contributors to your case and the relationship they have with the subject matter (for example, their standing within the organisation). Put another way, if you are examining, for example, the marketing of a particular product within an organisation but are reliant exclusively on details provided by the organisation's Finance office or by secondary data derived from published trade press resources rather than information provided directly through interviews with the marketing team, then how reliable is this data? Furthermore, with what authority does your case enable you to make generalisations and inferences that have applicability in other contexts? These questions of credibility, once again, draw attention to a strong focus in your methodology to ensure you can argue the adequacy of the choices you make in your research design and to enable you to make reasoned inferences in your analysis of the case data.

12.4 DEFINING THE BOUNDARIES OF YOUR CASE

Yin proposes that there are five components of research designs:

1. A case study's questions
2. Its propositions
3. Its case(s)
4. The logic linking the data to the propositions
5. The criteria for interpreting the findings[25]

Appraising these five components will help you to determine the boundaries for your research. Simons uses the term "bounded system" when exploring case boundaries. In other words, what is the single unit of analysis that you are going to select, citing examples such as a class, institution, project or programme? Once you've determined this, it is proposed that you can then begin to consider how this relates to the five components listed above. While a logical approach to your research might start by attempting to determine this bounded system, there are other techniques that adopt a more iterative approach to boundary setting for which the single best unit for analysis might be determined later after you have started your data gathering process. As Simons asserts "boundaries may also shift in the course of conducting the study and once you begin the analysis."[26] You may need to have gathered some data first before realising the preferred field, focus or perspective that will best enable you to address your case study's questions and/or propositions.

There are, of course, all sorts of practical factors that will impact on boundary setting including things like time, available funds, location of the research, number of potential contacts within viable organisations, and a willingness of organisational links to agree to participation. It is quite common to begin a project assuming all likely doors will be open, and respondents will be more than willing to engage with your research, but there are all sorts of practical reasons why this might not be the case. Don't be demoralised if not all your requests for interviews are received positively. Some respondents may receive such requests with suspicion or concern for the likely impact, for example, on the company's external reputation or its commercial sensitivities; or, as is most commonly the case, people simply don't have sufficient available time to engage in your case research aspirations. This may require a redefining of the boundaries to ensure adequate engagement to achieve your research objectives.

Other boundary considerations will include how many different respondents from within a single case organisation will you need to interview to ensure an adequate data set from which to develop your case narrative? And, where a multiple case strategy is being deployed, then how many cases from how many organisations are adequate to enable you to undertake meaningful comparative studies, draw analytical generalisations and/or formal causal inferences. There is normally a conceived tipping point beyond which any additional cases contribute little additional value to the overall research exercise, but this saturation figure can vary depending on the nature and complexity of the investigation and the breadth and depth of each case study narrative.

12.5 IN SUMMARY

In summary, this chapter has:

- introduced a glossary of terms for the case method in qualitative research, from the case as a research *strategy*, to the use of the case for *analytical generalisations, causal inferences* and for *theory-engaging congruence analysis*;
- considered the merits of different case techniques, involving either single- or multi-case approaches;
- identified components of case research design;
- provided guidance on boundary setting for case design.

The next chapter adopts a more practical tone as we explore approaches to gathering case data and the hurdles to be overcome.

NOTES

1 Denzin and Lincoln, 2018, p10.
2 Yin, 2004, pxii.
3 Saunders, Lewis and Thornhill, 2016, p124.
4 Creswell and Poth, 2017.
5 Examples of how the case method have been developed as a qualitative research tool are explored further in Yin, 2004 and Bryman, 1989, 2004.
6 Yin, 1993, p13.
7 Bryman, 2015.
8 Schwandt and Gates, referenced in Denzin and Lincoln, 2018, p341.
9 Ragin and Becker, 1992.
10 Flyvbjerg, referenced in Denzin and Lincoln, 2018, p315.
11 Gerring, 2004, p342.
12 Patton, 2002.
13 Stake, 2000, p23.
14 Willis, 2014, p4.
15 Bryman, 2015.
16 Yin, 2009, p54.
17 May, 2011, p226.
18 Yin, 2018, p26.
19 Gomm, Hammersley and Foster, 2000, p5.
20 Yin, 2018, p21.
21 Bennett and Elman, 2010, pp505–506.
22 Brady and Collier, 2004.
23 Gomm, Hammersley and Foster, 2000, p239.
24 Blatter and Blume, 2008, p316.
25 Yin, 2018, p27.
26 Simons, 2009, p29.

CHAPTER 13

How Do I Gather My Own Case Data?

This chapter explores approaches to gathering case data to ensure that your research objectives are fulfilled and that insights from participants are utilised effectively to contribute to the development of your case in both an ethical and impactful manner and, where appropriate, with the formal release authorisation of the organisation under review.

Whether you are planning to work with a single case or a number of cases, in order to report effectively on the data captured by your case(s), you will need to establish a clear *critical evaluation criteria* that will take account of all the issues that need to be explored within your research objectives. In establishing these 'evaluation criteria', it is important to ensure the following issues are considered:

1. Soundness and accuracy of analysis
2. Legitimacy
3. Range and evaluation of alternatives
4. Appropriateness and specificity of any recommendations
5. Consistency of logic[1]

Case studies are useful tools for qualitative research in complex organisations as they are concerned with the complexity and particular nature of a situation or organisation.[2] Bryman identified a number of illustrations of cases that have been undertaken to explore a single organisation[3] as well as cases for a single community, a single school and a single event. Cases often ensure that significant attention is drawn to the setting of the organisation or, to place this in management terms, the 'non-controllable environments' that surround organisations.[4]

Evaluation criteria take many different forms. For example, Guba and Lincoln developed evaluation criteria for qualitative research based on trustworthiness, using terms such as credibility, transferability, dependability and confirmability;[5] while Schroeder et al. studying innovations considered more prescriptive criteria where case research is deployed to showcase sequencing of activities. One example of how the critical evaluation has been established to determine a case strategy can be found in the agribusiness work described by Bitsch, who explores an analysis of seven case studies which were based on interviews and archival information from companies developing new innovations. As a result of this analysis, an adaptation to an innovation model was developed.[6] When

DOI: 10.4324/9781003345978-18

considering appropriate evaluation criteria to apply to this study, the more prescriptive objectives that were set were shaped around a sequence of activities during the development and implementation of new ideas. In another research project exploring the relationship between leadership and organisational growth among large churches, three primary evaluation criteria were set for the eight case organisations that contributed to the study:

- A minimum membership of 700 individuals.
- A record of sustained growth over a ten-year period.
- Each case organisation deployed a distinctly different organisational model.[7]

In each of these scenarios specific evaluation criteria ensure the case strategy has appropriate boundaries

13.1 SELECTING THE RIGHT NUMBER OF CASES

Having established your evaluation criteria, decisions then need to be taken about how many case investigations you will undertake to provide a credible and trustworthy response to your research questions and from who (or what) from within each case study context you will be drawing data.

Case studies commonly contain a combination of primary data from interviews or focus groups accompanied by secondary or archival, supporting data. Let's imagine you are looking to write your case on the actions of a specific organisation. You will need to determine who, from within the organisation, is best positioned to provide you with the types of data (evidence) that you require and what additional data you might be able to access from other secondary sources. It makes good sense to start with this secondary data as compiling these findings will help you to determine where the gaps are that need to be addressed through your primary research questions. For example, it is pointless asking a company director fact-finding questions about 'profit and loss' data for their respective organisation, when such information is already available in the company reports that are often freely accessible in the public domain. However, it might be perfectly reasonable to then use your knowledge of this data to explore 'why' the company is in this financial position and 'how' the director is planning to respond to the company's current financial situation. These 'how' and 'why' questions are commonly attributed to primary research objectives with the case method.

Secondary data sources could include company websites, published accounts and end-of-year reports, marketing material or third-party commentaries on the company such as trade press and news accounts.

It is quite common practice to interview more than one source from within the organisation to capture your primary data as this will ensure you derive a broader and more representative view of the area to which you are focusing your research. This is even more important if you are focusing your research strategy on a single case. For example, let's imagine you are investigating performance trends in a city hospital, using a single case approach, you may plan to capture data from a range of different resources representing a cross section of different departments from within the organisation to provide sufficient evidence to enable you to develop analytical generalisations.

When a researcher is studying different departments from within the same single case organisation there is scope for some generalisations to be developed from that single organisation. By contrast, as Baxter and Jack point out, when the researcher is studying multiple cases, the objective tends to be more focused towards developing a greater understanding of the differences and the similarities between the cases,[8] and the researcher has a greater capacity to analyse data from both within each case and across different case scenarios.

For such multiple case study strategies, the first question you may wish to ask is how many cases should I select? There are differing views on this and clearly the number will, in part, be determined by the nature of the research objectives, the context(s) within which the research is focused and the likely availability or willingness of viable participants to engage with the research. Eisenhardt argues, for example, that for theoretical coverage somewhere between four and ten cases is recommended.[9] A comparative research study from the Academy of Business, Engineering and Science at Halmstad University in Sweden compared the merits and pitfalls of either deploying a single or multiple case approach to your research.[10] The study draws comparative data from ten single case projects and from ten multi case strategies, and concludes that single case study strategies tend to be less expensive and time consuming compared to multiple case studies. From a value perspective single case studies tended to perform better when developing high-quality theory where the writer is forced to develop a deeper understanding of the exploring subject. Similarly single case studies can describe an in-depth exploration of the existence of specific phenomenon. By contrast the study concluded that multiple case study strategies provide opportunities for researchers to analyse case data within each situation and across different situations. Multiple cases provide a framework to understand similarities and differences between like-type or contrasting contexts and the evidence derived from multiple case studies tend to be considered as more credible, more reliable or trustworthy. As Gerring asserts, the more case studies found within a scientific article, the greater likelihood that it is confident in its representativeness but by contrast it is noted that there is likely to have been less case observation time adopted by the researcher.[11]

13.2 PROJECT EXAMPLES

To help us evaluate how many cases to deploy and how this links to capturing sufficient data to ensure credibility when developing a multiple case approach, let's look at three distinct research projects.

Project One – Domestic Appliances

First, we shall look at a project undertaken by Bressanelli, Perona and Saccani who investigated 'Challenges in supply chain redesign for the circular economy'. The research was published as a literature review with accompanying data from multiple case studies.[12] The case studies were based on companies engaged in the household appliance supply chain and comprised data from contributors at different stages of the supply chain to explore how companies tackle a range of supply chain challenges. The resultant analysis of the case data enabled the researchers to develop a theoretical framework (an inductive approach). The authors first used the literature review to provide the context and foundation for their primary research. If we take Yin's proposed five components of research design that we explored in the previous chapter, then we can apply this as follows:

1. **A case study's questions** – as the title of their paper implies, the general questions applied to this research explore the challenges in supply chain redesign in the content of the circular economy. Remember, case strategies tend to work well when exploring responses to 'how' and 'why' questions. In this research project two objectives were set, first *how* to categorise CE challenges for supply chain redesign and second *how* certain 'levers' could be used to overcome these challenges.

2. **Its propositions** – the study proposed that there are 24 challenges that may hamper a supply chain redesign for the circular economy.[13]

3. **Its case(s)** – four companies involved in the supply of washing machines were identified to provide the primary data for their case research strategy. In each company the data was captured through two or three interviews with CEO's and managers, with ten interviews being conducted in total.

4. **The logic linking the data to the propositions** – the researchers chose to adopt what they referred to as a *judgemental sampling technique* and the primary evaluation criteria adopted by the researchers when determining the appropriate contexts for their case selection were:

   a. Cases should concern companies having undertaken a circular economy (CE) project, involving the redesign of their value and/or supply chain;

   b. Cases should provide an adequate representation of different life cycle phases, supply chain actors, and altogether cover four CE building blocks (previously identified from the literature review).

   The four selected case studies were therefore considered on the basis that when considered together they provided data that presented a progressive journey through the domestic appliance supply chain.

5. **The criteria for interpreting the findings** – clearly four case studies will not provide statistically relevant data but, by adopting an approach that involved a company survey followed by selected in-company interviews, the researchers were able to explore the degree to which the 24 challenges identified from their literature review had occurred in each specific case.

Project Two – New Product Innovations

Second, we shall look at a project undertaken by Reinhardt, Gurtner and Griffin who investigated 'low-end innovation capability' in order to develop an adaptive framework. Once again, this research was informed by a systematic literature review to establish the best dimensions for their research and then this was followed with data from multiple case studies.[14]

On this occasion seven cases were used to inform their research objectives. Their resultant literature review concluded that "low-end innovation is organized around five disparate research streams, each of which offers a different perspective and emphasizes different success factors."[15]

When it came to determining the selection criteria for their cases, these researchers noted that by including cases from different markets and organisational contexts this would strengthen the external validity and generalisability of the case strategy. So they chose to include both established companies and new entrants, all of whom had been engaged in low-end innovations targeting developed and emerging markets. To further extend the range of contexts within these criteria, they selected companies that they considered to have engaged with both successful, partially successful and failed low-end innovations, noting that this range would likely increase the internal validity of their case strategy. As they approached each organisation, they first identified secondary data on each organisation from newspapers, magazines and blogs. Then, they interviewed key people from within the organisation (normally the CEOs or project managers); and finally, they supplemented each case narrative with secondary content derived from company reports, business plans and their websites. As Table 13.1 indicates, for each organisation there was at least one and as many as four separate interviews conducted, with 15 interviews being conducted in total.

This table provides a helpful illustration of the types of factors that you might wish to consider when determining your approach to capturing data. You will note from this table that the researchers have considered features including distinguishing geographic location, firm size, sector, target markets, data sources and number of interviews per case organisation, all of which are considered to be contributory factors in determining a case strategy from which to ensure adequate scope for generalisations. Drawing from a combination of the findings from the systematic literature review and the case study analysis, the researchers were able to conclude that successful low-end innovation results from building and orchestrating a diverse set of practices and processes which they were able to subsequently list. These, along with other findings enabled the research team to develop what they referred to as a low-end innovation capability framework.

Project Three – Management Accounting Functions

Thirdly, we look at a project undertaken by Lambert and Sponem who investigated 'roles, authority and involvement of the management accounting function'. Unlike the previous two, this research project did not set out to develop a particular theory or framework but rather sought to determine particular styles of management accounting function (*how*), each of which was associated with some form of 'role' related primarily to behaviour, power and control (*why*). Unlike the relatively low number of interviews conducted in the previous projects, this multiple case project involved 95 interviews and was based around 12 divisions of ten very large multinational companies, covering a range of different industrial sectors.[16] In addition to these interviews the researchers gathered additional secondary data from websites, internal documents and annual reports. Interestingly, the researchers also produced a 50-page case transcript based on three days of the work shadowing observations of a business management accountant, which they used to triangulate source data. Bitsch explores the merits of data triangulation – utilising multiple data sources – for case research commenting that it provides "an additional way to strengthen a study design" and supports "case credibility and confirmability."[17] She identifies three other types of triangulation commonly considered in case methodologies in addition to data triangulation,

TABLE 13.1 Overview of Cases and Data

Name	Firm size	Firm location	Innovations	Target Market	Success	Data	# of interviews	Informants
EnergyDev	Small	Advanced country (US)	Energy products	Emerging markets	Low-end NPD is perceived as much harder and slower than high-end NPD. Not yet able to launch a low-end innovation successfully.	Interviews, business plans, newspaper articles	4	CEO, Founder and Head of R&D, BD Manager, NGO partner
BrightLight	Small	Advanced country (US)	Lighting devices	Emerging markets	Several successful low-end innovations.	Interviews, newspaper articles	2	Founder and CEO
MedTech	Small	Emerging country (India)	Medical devices	Emerging markets	Low-end medical device successfully launched.	Interviews, newspaper articles	2	Founder and CEO
SightSee	Small	Advanced country (EU)	Mobile tourism app	Developed markets	New product failed and the firm filed for bankruptcy.	Interviews, business plans, blogs, newspaper articles	2	CEO and Lead Engineer, BD Manager
CloudHome	Small	Advanced country (EU)	Cloud computing and smart home devices	Developed markets	Several products launched successfully but desired market penetration not yet achieved.	Interview, observation, business plans, newspaper articles	1	Founder and CTO

(continued)

TABLE 13.1 (Continued)

Name	Firm size	Firm location	Innovations	Target Market	Success	Data	# of interviews	Informants
HealthDev1	Large	Multi-national, R&D in both emerging and advanced countries	Medical devices	Emerging markets	Product not yet launched but satisfactory progress in NPD and tests.	Interviews, newspaper articles	3	CMO, Project Manager
HealthDev2	Large	Multi-national, R&D primarily in emerging country	Medical devices	Emerging markets	Several successful low-end innovations launched.	Interviews, newspaper articles	1	Project Manager

Notes: CEO – Chief Executive Officer; CTO – Chief Technology Officer; CMO – Chief Marketing Officer; BD – Business Development Manager; NGO – Non-Governmental Organisation

Source: Table 4, p778 from Reinhardt, R., Gurtner, S., and Griffin, A. (2018) Towards an Adaptive Framework of Low-end Innovation Capability: A Systematic Review and Multiple Case Study Analysis. *Long Range Planning* 51(5), pp770–796. https://doi.org/10.1016/j.lrp.2018.01.004. Reproduced by permission.

these are investigator triangulation (utilising more than one researcher), theory triangulation (relating case data sets to multiple perspectives to test and explore different explanations) and methodological triangulation (drawing from numerous methodological approaches to address the same problem or case).

While it might be reasonable to assume at first glance that this latter research project achieves greater trustworthiness by virtue of its extensive number of interviews, the authors are quick to note that one of their perceived limitations of the research is the data collection method. Given that these cases provide in-depth examinations of ten companies spread across a wide range of contexts – both geographical and by sector – the authors considered that they offer only a limited capacity for wider generalisation.

Even within these three project examples we can see a range of approaches adopted to data capture which informs case design and this shines a light on some of the complexities of choosing the right options when determining your own approach to case data capture.

13.3 MAKE THE FIRST CONNECTION WITH THE CASE ORGANISATION

Having determined which organisation you wish to use as your participating case, the next step is to make first contact and determine *who* from within the organisation you will be inviting to contribute to your case and in *what capacity*. Having determined who you wish to participate, then your first contact and introduction should enable you to explain the purpose of the research and to determine both the parameters and the boundaries of the research. In general, you as the researcher will wish to clarify the parameters of your research (i.e., what areas of the organisation's activities are of interest to your research in order to enable you to address the key project objectives), and a representative of the organisation commonly agrees the boundaries of the research, which might include who you can interview, what types of questions are permissible and what information can or cannot be shared. Agreeing these points in advance is an important function of case planning and preparation and without this level of agreement you will be in danger of pursuing goals beyond the permissible remit of the participants, which might lead to future legal challenges to the release of case data. Any sensitive data is likely to require prior approval of release authorisation from the organisation's legal representative and this should be an early priority of the research team to safeguard your project's integrity and guard against any future challenge. This process of agreeing the ground rules for the case research will improve the likelihood of a smooth-flowing, data-capture process.

If you are based within a university or similar research organisation, then it is likely that you will already have an organisational ethics policy for conducting research. It is important to familiarise yourself with this policy to ensure you are operating within its constraints as you prepare to engage with the host organisation. This might include full initial disclosure of the purpose and/or objectives of the research along with a full list of all the intended interview questions. Other requirements might include signed consent and a written agreement that participation is entirely voluntary and that participants may wish to freely withdraw at any point from the research process.

13.4 PREPARING INTERVIEWS

Your interview style needs to be determined as part of the planning process. You may have a rigid pre-agreed collection of questions that you are planning to use and, where appropriate, to replicate for each consecutive case in your study. This approach does provide consistency for comparative purposes, but it can hinder the flow of a conversation and potentially cause you to miss out on certain specific areas of discovery that will be unique to each individual case participant. A loose, in-depth, or less-structured interviewing approach might allow you to derive a deeper level of understanding of what the participant actually thinks and how they perceive their organisational issues from their own perspective. This approach is more likely to encourage active engagement with the interviewee to enhance the overall learning potential for the interview. As you begin to consider your own approach to conducting an interview then you may need to consider in advance whether to adopt a formal or personal interviewing approach. This will no doubt depend, in part, on your familiarity with the interviewee or their organisation and its context. There are pros and cons for each approach and so you will need to develop a style that both you and your interviewee are most comfortable with if you are to develop a conversational flow that will allow you to elicit the deepest level of honest participation from your interviewee.

For many interviewers their principal aim is to adopt a style that puts the interviewee at ease and allows the discussion to flow as if it were an informal conversation. In addition to the structured and unstructured/in-depth approaches to interviews highlighted above, Saunders, Lewis and Thornhill also draw attention to semi-structured interviews, which tend to be more shaped around a collection of themes rather than a rigid set of questions and for which they suggest:

> the interview schedule for this type of interview will also be likely to contain some comments to open the discussion, a possible list of prompts to promote any further discussion, and some comments to close it.[18]

Such semi-structured interviews are commonly adopted as the preferred approach when developing case research as they enable the interviewer to not only explore explanations related to the case proposition but also to elicit insights related to personal views including attitudes, perceptions, opinions and feelings. Heath reflects on the emphasis of different personal views provided while conducting case research, noting that *opinions can often be far more important than facts* when determining the decision-making process for organisations.[19] Yin also comments that improper data capture can be a weakness of drawing from interviews for case data as inaccuracies can occur when there is poor recall after the event.[20]

Regardless of which interviewing approach you choose to adopt, it would be advisable to agree with the interviewee that the interview is recorded to enable you to accurately transcribe the responses after the interview has concluded. Heath draws attention to the perils of attempting to take notes during a case interview process and the likelihood of such an action appearing to intimidate the interviewee.[21] Recording can be managed in a less obtrusive manner and often proves to be essential for certain types of analysis of case data to ensure an accurate and specific capture of case responses from each participant. It is advisable to transcribe the text from a recording as soon as possible after the interview to ensure that the comments align with the themes that you were intending to explore and to avoid confusion when working with multiple data sources (i.e., different contributors).

13.5 ALTERNATIVES TO INTERVIEWS FOR CASE DATA CAPTURE

Yin points out that one of the weaknesses of adopting an interview approach to case data capture could be interviewee bias, albeit some of this can be avoided with carefully constructed questioning. Another weakness might be what he refers to as "reflexivity – e.g. Interviewee says what interviewer wants to hear."[22] One approach to mitigate against this might be to adopt a more prologued interview approach whereby each participant agrees to a number of different interviews conducted over a longer period of time. If this was to be conducted over several sittings, then each time you meet with the interviewee you can elicit information about their opinions and viewpoints in relation to the case situation and then use their feedback as the basis for the further enquiry. Yin notes that the more an interviewee engages in this approach, the more they become seen as an *informant* rather than a participant. However, the peril remains that over the course of cultivating that interviewer–informant relationship, the interviewee may become more inclined to provide a response that they perceive the interviewer is seeking.

This therefore invites you to consider whether there might be more preferable alternative sources of data from which you could capture evidence that provides greater trustworthiness and authenticity. These might be from archival evidence (or secondary data) or direct observations in the workplace. This latter suggestion works best where the theme under review within the case is not historic but rather it continues to present itself within an organisational context. This provides the opportunity to consider establishing some form of observational approach either through gathering video-recorded evidence or by literally positioning yourself in the workplace (shadowing) in order to capture observational data. This does, of course, require significant permission-granting on the part of the case organisation, and this can sometimes be time-consuming and cost-prohibitive.

Most often these concerns about the trustworthiness of interview data can be mitigated against by drawing insights from more than one contributor, either conducted as a collection of individual interviews or as a focus group. A focus group tends to draw together a small number of participants for a group interview, facilitated by a moderator. Over and above individual participant responses, Morgan draws attention to the additional benefits of group interaction with focus groups, which he defines as "the explicit use of group interaction to provide data and insights that would be less accessible without the interactions found in the group."[23]

If the group is to be effective, then the themes or context for the case should be clearly defined beforehand as this then enables the moderator to focus the group's time on an interactive discussion between the respective participants. Focus groups tend to work best with either semi-structured or in-depth interviews.

Gratton and O'Donnell provide some interesting insights as an example of using case focus groups as a means of gaining buy-in from First Nations (Aboriginal) Canadians who had previously been reluctant to participate in research with non-Aboriginal researchers, given feelings of scepticism and distrust towards them. The researchers therefore needed to adopt an approach that would allow participants to "be more deeply involved in the process."[24] The decision to use case focus groups proved to be a favourable participatory research approach with this subject group, as they were empowered to become more collaborative in their involvement in the research, to "voice their opinions, share their knowledge, and have more control over every step of the research process."[25] On this occasion, due to the large geographic spread of the participants, the focus groups took place remotely by using multi-site videoconferencing technology. A sample group of 30 participants were invited to join the focus groups, from which 22 respondents engaged with the research and formed five focus groups in total. Each group session lasted about two hours, was videorecorded and the transcripts were then used for case analysis. The researchers noted that not only was this approach helpful in terms of gaining the trust of the participating group, but it also saved considerably on research costs. There were, however, some noticeable limitations to a study of this nature as the researchers noted that not being physically face-to-face in the same room as the participants may have influenced their mood and created an atmosphere different to that which might have been achieved with an in-person focus group.

By contrast, Yelland and Gifford explored the use of focus groups as a function of case study research in the management of health education research, more specifically exploring the problems faced with using focus groups to study beliefs about sudden infant death syndrome. They aimed to develop three focus groups each involving 6–8 participants from each of nine ethnic groups, eventually developing 23 groups drawing on support from 104 contributors in total. Having garnered initial support for the research through various networks, the project-leads then provided each participant with a fuller explanation of the research to gain informed consent prior to the one-hour face-to-face focus group sessions. The researchers commented on a *theme list* that was utilised to ensure particular emphasis was placed on key areas pertinent to their case research.[26] Because of the sensitive nature of the subject matter, the researchers noted that there were significant pitfalls when it came to recruiting candidates and ensuring their buy-in, with most respondents commonly suggesting a preference to conduct the research as individual interviews rather than in a group context. It was nonetheless noted that once the group had gathered, in what was an intentionally informal and relaxing environment, then as soon as one participant opened up to share their experiences, others felt more encouraged to offer their own views. The researchers also noted that in some situations the focus groups were dominated by one or two key respondents and so others may have felt intimidated or less able to openly share their own views. The willingness to engage and share opening within the focus group contexts appeared to be largely influenced by the level of familiarity between the group members.

These contrasting pictures shed insights into some of the complexities of organising your interviews or focus groups to ensure adequate, credible and trustworthy data is captured to inform your case analysis. And while secondary archive data provides a useful contrast to interview data, in reality most case strategies tend to deploy a combination of these approaches to qualitative data capture, as indicated in the three project examples from earlier in this chapter. The expectation is that by combining data sources this provides greater scope for eradicating bias or extreme viewpoints and cross references anecdotal evidence with published content.

13.6 IN SUMMARY

In summary, this chapter has:

- demonstrated the importance of establishing clear *critical evaluation criteria* prior to case selection;
- compared three different strategies of multi-case study research;
- explored the challenges of developing a case-based approach to data capture through structured, semi-structured and unstructured/in-depth interviews;
- provided contrasting examples of the use of focus groups as a mechanism for capturing data based on group interaction.

Having explored data capture for your case research, the next chapter considers options for analysing your case data.

NOTES

1 Ellet, 2018, pp48–49; Mauffette-Leenders, Erskine and Leenders, 2007, p100.
2 Stake, 1995.
3 See Bryman, 2004; Similar examples are also discussed by Burawoy, 1979; Pollert, 1981; Cavendish, 1982; Pettigrew, 1985.
4 See the models conceptualised in Kotler and Keller, 2008; similar models are also explored in Johnson and Scholes, 1993.
5 Guba and Lincoln, 1989.
6 Bitsch, 2005.
7 Andrews, 2015.
8 Baxter and Jack, 2008.
9 Eisenhardt, 1989.
10 Gustafsson, 2017.
11 Gerring, 2004.
12 Bressanelli, Perona and Saccani, 2019.
13 Ibid, p7397.
14 Reinhardt, Gurtner and Griffin, 2018.
15 Ibid, p774.
16 Lambert and Sponem, 2012.
17 Bitsch, 2005, p84.

18 Saunders, Lewis and Thornhill, 2016, p391.

19 Heath, 2015, p79.

20 Yin, 2018.

21 Heath, 2015, p55.

22 Yin, 2018, p114.

23 Morgan, 1988, p12.

24 Gratton and O'Donnell, 2011, p164.

25 Ibid.

26 Yelland and Gifford, 1995.

CHAPTER 14

How Do I Analyse and Draw Conclusions from My Own Case Data?

Having gathered the case data and formatted your case(s) there are several qualitative approaches that you could adopt to analyse the data against the key research question(s) of your project. This chapter begins by examining the merits of each of these analytical approaches. Having gathered and analysed your case data, the next step is to interpret these findings considering the overall objectives of the project, to consider their contribution to knowledge and to determine the transferrable value of such findings.

> The term case study is often taken to carry implications for the kind of data that are collected, and perhaps also for how these are analysed. Frequently, but not always, it implies the collection of unstructured data, and qualitative analysis of those data.[1]

The case method is heuristic in that it is a self-guided learning opportunity that employs analysis to help draw conclusion about situations. Data can be extracted from a single case or a selection of cases to provide opportunities for comparisons and contrasts. These can then be evaluated to promote opinion forming. However different readers may adopt different opinions according to how they choose to treat the case.[2] So how do you analyse your case data? And what conclusions might you meaningfully expect to draw from such potentially unstructured data? These questions need to be considered before you start your research strategy as they arguably need to be informed by your selected research questions.

In Gustafsson's review of the case method in research,[3] it is suggested that case studies can be used by researchers to test theories,[4] to provide a descriptive analysis,[5] and to develop theory about many different topics including, for example, themes related to the internal organisation,[6] group processes,[7] and strategy.[8]

When considering how to structure a report based on case study research, you will need to reflect on how you used this research strategy. First, is the purpose of your case study research designed to be descriptive, exploratory, explanatory or evaluative? Second, is your case study research to be based on a deductive, inductive or abductive approach?[9]

DOI: 10.4324/9781003345978-19

Yin argues that all these types of cases can be useful and serve valid purposes but that the right approach should be measured against what he refers to as three conditions:

1. The form of research question that is posed.
2. The control that you as the research have over the events of the case.
3. The degree to which the case focuses on contemporary rather than historic events.[10]

In contrast to other well-established research methods, the case study does not require control over the events to which you are researching, but the focus on contemporary events is likely to be important if the situation is to be accurately captured and analysed. Let's explore each of these four types of purpose for your case study in turn, considering how each might then be used to promote opportunities for analysis.

14.1 DESCRIPTIVE RESEARCH

A case study that is there to support a descriptive approach is one that requires both focus and detail. The case situation or scenario would normally be carefully explored and critically reviewed and any subsequent expression of what is known about the situation or scenario may be referred to as descriptive theory. Put another way, descriptive research can incorporate many different approaches to data collection and the case method is considered to be one of them.

Descriptive case studies tend to attempt to define a real-world problem and provide essential facts about it. They often describe the key people and/or groups involved in the problem and their actions, behaviours, thoughts and opinions. The relationships between these people (the 'actors') and the events that they encounter is captured and the actors' perceptions of the problem or situation and any solutions that they might choose are also summarised. The descriptive case might include an analysis and evaluation of the chosen solution, its implementation and the outcomes.

Simons explores what she terms a *descriptive narrative observation* approach to case analysis, which is based on a three-step process of listen, look and document. She notes that in such description observational research there are three things that matter: the context, the timing and the close description.[11] In most cases, descriptive narrative observation is captured after the event and might commonly involve three components: a close description of the facts, an observation of the emotions and behavioural responses (which might therefore also inform opinions and motives) and the subsequent decisions (actions) that are taken. This is commonly practised in medical and healthcare research and there are plenty of examples of patient observations being recorded to note new responses, reactions and behaviours towards practices in healthcare management. Remember, the case method is often adopted when looking to address 'how' and 'why' questions, so it is worth considering how descriptive analysis can serve to address these same types of questions.

Similarly, Yin refers to a special type of observation achieved by what he refers to as *participant observation*, where you as the researcher are in some way actively involved (or practising) as part of the observation or fieldwork situation.[12] Yin explores an example of researching a particular neighbourhood by actually agreeing to live there or adopting a specific functional role within the neighbourhood to assume a different perspective on the subject under investigation. This approach is commonly adopted in studies of different cultural or social groups and is not limited to scientific anthropology but rather can include the culture of a specific organisation or a business environment.

One type of descriptive approach is commonly referred to as *thick description*. Thomas refers to this as "understanding a piece of behaviour – a nod, a word, a pause for example – in context, and using one's 'human knowing' to interpret it when one describes it."[13] When teaching a case study as part of a class discussion (as was pointed out in previous sections of this book), students are often invited to step *into the shoes of* the protagonist. Similarly, in thick description, you are invited to imagine yourself in the shoes of the participant (subject) and from that personalised perspective, to reflect, to imagine and to interpret what is happening. By stepping into the shoes of the participant you are not only describing what you hear revealed at an interview, but you are also experiencing and observing the world from the context that they inhabit. As such, thick description can be a much more immersive approach to case research.

There are different approaches to structuring your case study, but descriptive cases tend to work in linear-analytical, comparative, chronological and unsequenced-type structures, but are less useful for theory-building or suspense-building cases.

Wherever possible, you should have considered how to order your descriptive framework before starting data collection, to ensure that the collection is purposive to meet the analytical opportunities presented by your framework. However, in some scenarios a descriptive approach may have emerged as an analytic strategy if you are having difficulty formulating how else you might use the case data. Only after completing the data capture and the framing of the case structure might it then become clearer whether the case could also serve additional *exploratory* or *explanatory* purposes, as detailed in the next section.

14.2 EXPLORATORY RESEARCH

Exploratory case study research investigates distinct phenomena often characterised in scenarios where there might be a lack of detailed preliminary research or formulated hypotheses that can be tested.[14]

One example of exploratory case research can be found in a study of online instructors engaged in educational management. Research from the University of Saskatchewan explored data relating to 12 online instructors, which was used as the basis for an investigation into *factors associated with instructor engagement*.[15] Feedback on the experiences of 12 online instructors were examined over a one-year period. Each instructor was interviewed and both positive and negative experiences were captured along with their frequency of occurrence. The exploratory study set out to explore what factors affect faculty engagement when faculty teach online and what the potential barriers were to their engagement. In their own explanation of their choice of research strategy, the researchers noted "this was an exploratory study designed to inform the direction of a larger quantitative study. Because the study was exploratory and not suited to the testing of a hypothesis, the researchers adopted a grounded theory methodological framework."[16] The *facts* related to the situations facing each participant were captured in the case study alongside the *opinions* and *behaviours* of the participants, which informed the qualitative analysis, and which was principally measured by the number of positive and negative experiences discussed by participants. The analysis of this data was based on the assumption that instructors who were more engaged would exhibit a positive mindset related to their online courses and those less engaged would most likely exhibit feelings of detachment and cynicism.

This case research approach could be described as *exploratory* on the basis of the small number of participants and that the findings had limited generalisability but could nonetheless be used to inform a larger quantitative study. Exploratory case research can provide useful opportunities for opinion forming as the researchers noted that, after spending a year observing online instructors struggle and succeed, this did enable the researchers to develop their own opinions about how online instructors could be better supported.

These types of exploratory case studies are particularly useful when looking to determine an extensive or in-depth understanding of a social phenomenon, where there are potential causal links that are too complex to explore using a survey or experimental methodology. The focus for most exploratory studies is the setting of the 'what' question, as Yin explains:

> Some types of questions are exploratory, such as "What can be learnt from the study of a start-up business?" This type of question is a justifiable rationale for an exploratory study, the goal being to develop pertinent hypotheses and propositions for further enquiry.[17]

Exploratory case studies can be used as an approach for theory-building or theory-affirming. The theory-building approach involves using one or more cases to "create theoretical constructs, propositions, and/or midrange theory from case based, empirical evidence."[18] Whereas, by contrast *explanatory* case studies more commonly affirm an existing theory. In the previous chapter we explored the arguments for developing a multi-case study approach. Clearly, when seeking to build theory, the use of multiple case studies provides greater scope for comparison which can strengthen the argument of the theory-building process.

In summary, Thomas proposes four key components to an exploratory case study:

1. Initial fieldwork to gather facts.
2. Posing potential explanations or solutions.
3. Exploratory work to examine the likely viability of such explanations.
4. The testing of those explanations.[19]

Cases designed for exploratory purposes tend to favour one of the following structures: linear-analytical, comparative, chronological and theory-building, whereas exploratory case research is less popular for suspense-building or unsequenced-type case structuring.

14.3 EXPLANATORY RESEARCH

Explanatory case study research tends to be most valuable where it is testing data for its internal validity and often relates to research that is seeking to establish some form of *causal relationship* between certain conditions (i.e., where one condition or set of circumstances leads to another condition), and hence the analysis of the case data seeks to provide a causal explanation.

While exploratory cases often explore the 'what' questions, explanatory cases are more geared towards considering 'how' and 'why' questions, which tend to "deal with the tracing of operational processes over time rather than mere frequencies or incidence."[20]

Explanatory cases can therefore be adopted to test and apply theory or theories to a particular situation (or set of situations) to firmly demonstrate or argue the basis for key generalisations. These types of cases have frequently been adopted in business research as well as in public policy, urban planning and healthcare research.[21]

For example, the aptly titled 'Explaining the Cuban Missile Crisis', developed by Allison and Zelikow[22] provides an example of an explanatory case which draws from three well-established theories as part of a very large and complex case study involving tens of thousands of pages of evidence. The authors of the study compare the three presented theories to consider their capacity to adequately explain the full events of the crisis and they even include their own appraisal of lessons learnt from the case in contrast to previously held views of the study of war. In his review of this 'classic' case study, Yin attributes its success in part to its "sharpness of the research questions, contribution to theory and exhaustive review of evidence."[23] As these types of case studies are often used to attempt to explain complex and multi-faceted aspects of organisational practice or policy development, it is perhaps not surprising that they can become quite large cases formed from the analysis of large and complex data sets.

Of the six different approaches to structuring your case study, linear-analytical, comparative, chronological, theory-building and suspense-building cases all support explanatory type case research whereas unsequenced-type structures are less applicable.

14.4 EVALUATIVE RESEARCH

Whether your case design has been descriptive, exploratory or explanatory, all three can potentially then be analysed (or compared with other like-type cases) for the purpose of an evaluative study.

You might expect an evaluative case research approach to involve multiple case studies, and while this might be the most common approach, it is still feasible to construct a large and complex single case study for evaluative purposes. Such a case might be formed from multiple investigations into its processes or activities, for example a global business with many regional operations or a hospital with multiple departments. Multiple explorations, either through internal surveys or successive interviews would provide multiple units of data that can then be analysed for evaluative purposes. Scholars have mixed views of the appropriateness of using cases for evaluation purposes and those supporters of the method are also divided into whether or not they can be of value only when used as part of a wider study involving other research strategies, or the contrasting view that evaluations that are exclusively formed through a case method strategy provide an adequate evaluative response. The benefit of using a case strategy for evaluation is that they not only provide a set of results as a response to some form of analysis, but they can also serve a more holistic function to explore or explain the processes that were undertaken in the area under investigation that led to the outcomes that you have determined from your evaluation. This more holistic approach enables a fuller picture to be formed which, as has already been stated, explains both *how* and *why* such evaluations might have been formed.

Comparative evaluative studies tend to be most commonly adopted where a selection of cases have been developed or what some refer to as multi-case research. For example, Yin provides a frequently adopted theoretical framework for multi-case research which adopts a *replication* approach as a case strategy. Having developed the theory, selected the cases and designed how you are going to collect your data, Yin proposes that you then conduct your case study and write the individual case report before then moving on to the next case study and to write up your second report. As you continue through this process there is also a feedback loop to the study design, should there be any unanticipated discoveries in your research process that might cause you to rethink the theoretic proposition and/or redesign your thinking and approach before continuing. In this way the case development process evolves in an iterative manner over time. Having written each individual case report, the model then suggests you look to draw cross-case conclusions which might enable you to propose modifications to your theory before creating your overall cross-case report.[24]

In a US study examining the use of evaluative cases studies for USAID development projects, its report details the challenges for researchers of using two different processes when conducted a case evaluation with multiple case studies:

> First, they will analyze each case individually to understand it as a separate entity, as described above. After that, they will conduct a cross-case analysis, comparing and contrasting the results from the different cases. This process is similar to triangulation and also yields similar benefits: greater confidence in findings and the minimization of potential bias.[25]

The first challenge when developing cases for an evaluation approach is to determine the principal unit of analysis. This might be a particular individual that holds the same office (for example, the CEO), or a specific group (for example, the senior management team) from within each case. Some evaluative cases might consider larger groups or communities such as whole groups of employees or customers from whole regions.

While these types of evaluations enable a limited level of *generalisation*, it is argued that such results might not be rationalised as *statistically* relevant but might be considered to be feasible for some *analytical* generalisations where there is no need for a statistically representative sample of a larger population. The evaluation case works best when it focuses on an ongoing intervention or one recently completed, and where you have sufficient time within the case context for in-depth data collection. Often such cases are found where the data is complex and cannot be clearly separated from the context in which it is embedded.

The USAID review provides a useful checklist of questions to consider when determining your evaluative case approach, which can be summarised with the following questions:[26]

- Is the rationale clearly presented for use of the evaluation case study method?
- Is it clear which type of case study has been conducted?
- Is the unit of analysis clear?
- Is the justification clear for the number of case studies conducted?
- Is the rationale provided for the selection of the specific case(s) or site(s)?
- Is the context in which the intervention is embedded 'clearly' described?
- Are data collection methods within the case study clearly described?
- If a multi-site case study is undertaken, is there clear explanation of the within-site analyses and cross-site analysis?
- If an explanatory case study is undertaken, are alternative rival explanations for findings identified and examined?

There are arguably three types of data that can be derived for evaluative purposes and your choice of analysis will undoubtedly be shaped by the type of data that you are gathering:

1. **Historical data** can be analysed to present case findings through a chronological presentation of the case, similar to a narrative story.

2. Multiple **critical incidents** can be reported drawing data from individual situations that share a common feature using reports that captures similar data for evaluative purposes.

3. **Thematic analysis** is commonly adopted (often using a coding approach) when evaluating data from transcripts derived from multiple interviews. Subsequent case reports are organised around the key themes that have emerged from the case study, sometimes based on key evaluation criteria or questions.

Such analyses that involve multiple case studies might include evaluation reports based on data analysed both from within each specific case and between the cases. When writing up your research it is quite common to present the cross-case analysis within the main body of your report, while the individual case study summaries are included as annexes.

Case-based evaluations are often appropriate when evaluating complex interventions.[27] In complex interventions it may be very hard to find simple indicators that can provide evidence for desired changes, and the focus is often on unexpected and/or negative changes. Case-based evaluations can cope with complex change, as they do not rely on predefined indicators.

14.5 IN SUMMARY

Yin sums up case data analysis using "any combination of procedures, such as by examining, categorising, tabulating, testing, or otherwise recombining (narrative and numeric) evidence";[28] and he goes on to conclude:

> the best preparation for conducting case study analysis is to have a general analytic strategy. The purpose of the analytic strategy is to link your case study data to important concepts of interest, and then have the concepts give you a sense of direction in analyzing the data.[29]

So, whichever approach you chose to select to analyse your case data, the important thing you should remember is to ensure that you can argue the adequacy of your chosen analytical approach to achieve the objectives of your case strategy.

In summary, this chapter has:

- examined four potential purposes for your case study research: descriptive, exploratory, explanatory or evaluative;
- considered the merits of each of these purposes;
- aligned each purpose to different approaches to structuring your case study analysis;
- drawn from examples of published research.

NOTES

1 Gomm, Hammersley and Foster, 2000, p3.
2 Ellet, 2018; Heath, 2015.
3 Gustafsson, 2017, p4.
4 Anderson, 1983; Pinfield, 1986.
5 Kidder, 1982.
6 Gilbert, 2005; Galunic and Eisenhardt, 2001.
7 Edmondson, Bohmer and Pisano, 2001.
8 Mintzberg and Waters, 1982.
9 Saunders, Lewis and Thornhill, 2016, p646.
10 Yin 2018, p9.
11 Simons, 2009, p56.
12 Yin, 2018, p125.
13 Thomas, 2021, p233.
14 Mills, Durepos and Wiebe, 2010.
15 Seaton and Schwier, 2014.
16 Ibid, p4; see also Seale, 2006, pp239–248.
17 Yin, 2018, p10.
18 Eisenhardt and Graebner, 2007, p25.
19 Thomas, 2021, p141.
20 Yin, 2018, p10.

21 Fisher and Ziviani, 2004.
22 Allison and Zelikow, 2004.
23 Yin, 2004, p13.
24 Yin, 2018, pp57–58.
25 USAID, 2013, p7.
26 Ibid, p11.
27 Stern et al., 2012.
28 Yin, 2018, p164.
29 Ibid, p174.

SECTION E

Case Resources

This final section contains an informative chapter that provides details of the resources you can access to gain further insights about case studies, whether for class-based learning, projects and assignments, or for your research. External agencies from across the world that offer case study support and resources for both learning and research are outlined, and the References section lists all sources that have been used to inform this book.

DOI: 10.4324/9781003345978-20

CHAPTER 15

Further Resources to Support Case Development

This chapter provides signposting to other case-based organisations that can provide learning resources and further insights to aid your understanding of the case method both as a learner and as a researcher.

A broad range of organisations supporting case development have been captured in the previous chapters of this book, many of which are listed here. Unavoidably, the organisations listed, and the website links provided, are likely to change from time to time, so for more regular updates on these case development resources see the additional Support Material that accompanies this book, which can be found at www.routledge.com/9781032386324.

Asia Case Research Centre (ACRA), University of Hong Kong

www.acrc.hku.hk/

Formerly known as the Centre for Asian Business Cases, ACRA was established in 1997 and has developed a broad range of case-based resources (including multi-media cases) for wider circulation across Asia. ACRA runs an annual Asia Pacific Business Case Competition which attracts participants from across the world. The Centre also delivers case teaching workshops and case writing guides.

Asian Business Case Centre (ABCC), Nanyang Business School, Singapore

www.ntu.edu.sg/asiacase

ABCC was formed in 2000 to develop an Asian case repository with initial support from the Richard Ivey School of Business, Canada, paying special attention to entrepreneurship and innovation in the region. As well as holding a regional Asian Management Case Collection, it also delivers case training workshops and produces casebooks. Given its close proximity to China, ABCC has translated many cases into Chinese to broaden their appeal across Asia. It has established distribution partnerships with Harvard Business Publishing, Ivey Publishing and The Case Centre.

The Case Centre, UK and US

www.thecasecentre.org

Created in 1973, The Case Centre is the independent home of the case method. A not-for-profit organisation and registered charity, it is dedicated to advancing the case method worldwide. It was formerly known as the Case Clearing House of Great Britain and Ireland, and then the European Case Clearing House (ECCH). From its offices at Cranfield

DOI: 10.4324/9781003345978-21

University, UK and Babson College, US the organisation holds and distributes the world's largest and most diverse collection of management cases, articles, book chapters and teaching materials. This includes the collections of Harvard Business School, IBSCDC, INSEAD and Ivey Business School, among many others. Items are available in a range of different media and languages. Discover more about the collection at www.thecasecentre.org/cases.

To support case teachers, writers and learners The Case Centre also:

- delivers case workshops and webinars, www.thecasecentre.org/workshops
- runs case competitions, www.thecasecentre.org/starquality
- offers scholarships at www.thecasecentre.org/scholarships
- hosts Learning with Cases: An Interactive Study Guide, www.thecasecentre.org/guide.

The Case Development Centre, Rotterdam School of Management, the Netherlands
www.rsm.nl/cdc/
The Case Development Centre (CDC) was established in 2008 to support the development of case studies in management education by working alongside authors and organisations to produce high-quality teaching outputs including teaching notes and case competitions. They provide a range of learning resources to support the case writing process and hold their own case collection (see www.rsm.nl/cdc/case-catalogue/). Not only are cases developed for class-based learning, but they also work with individuals and businesses to develop cases to showcase good practice or for internal business training and development purposes.

Case Method Institute, Washington, USA
http://casemethodinstitute.com/
The Case Method Institute supports training and development programmes aimed at enhancing the capacity for individuals to hone their case teaching and writing skills, by offering a range of coaching and training services

China Europe International Business School (CEIBS), Shanghai, China
www.ceibs.edu/
The Case Development Centre at CEIBS was established in 2001 to provide a range of case resources with a specific focus on business in China. They have since partnered with the Harvard Case Library, Ivey Publishing and The Case Centre to provide wider distribution opportunities for its China-focused cases.

Darden Business Publishing, University of Virginia, USA
http://store.darden.virginia.edu/
The Darden case collection includes more than 3,000 cases, teaching notes and case articles. Darden established its publishing activities in 2003 and more recently has particularly invested in the development of multi-media and simulation cases. It is one of the largest publishers of case resources in the US. It has also produced a number of articles on the case writing and teaching process.

European Foundation for Management Development (EFMD), Brussels, Belgium
www.efmdglobal.org/
EFMD describes itself as a membership-driven, global network of almost 1,000 institutions from more than 90 institutions in six continents. They provide a world-renowned quality accreditation scheme and play host to an annual writing case competition.

Harvard Business Publishing, Cambridge, USA
https://store.hbr.org/
Arguably the home of the management case study. Harvard produced its first book of business and management case studies in 1921 and has been developing cases ever since. Harvard Case Studies are available to purchase for your own use from Harvard Business Publishing and their collection also includes books, teaching bundles, multimedia resources and business simulations, articles and magazine issues. Harvard also host competitions (see www.thecasecompetition.org/) and run a regular open programme of case teaching and writing workshops both at its base in Cambridge and at centres cross the world. One particular resource for students that was showcased in this book is Harvard's Interactive Introduction to Case Study Analysis (see https://hbsp.harvard.edu/product/7886-HTM-ENG).

IBS Case Development Centre (IBS CDC), Hyderabad, India
http://ibscdc.org/
IBS CDC boasts Asia Pacific's largest case collection for business and management, including bestselling and award-winning cases, case books and case packs (including cases, teaching notes and structured assignments). IBS CDC was launched in 2003 and has developed a repository of more than 5,500 cases including multi-media case and movie-based cases.

IE Publishing, IE Business School, Madrid, Spain
https://iepublishing.ie.edu/en/
IE Business School has been actively promoting the case method for more than 40 years and has developing a publishing outlet for development and circulation of case studies. More recently it has invested significantly in the development of multi-media, simulations and online case studies. IE manages a case catalogue and hosts an annual case contest.

IMD, Lausanne, Switzerland and Singapore
www.imd.org/
With over 50 years' experience of developing cases, IMD is one of the leading case producing institutions to emerge from Europe. Now with a second campus in Singapore, IMD has looked to develop, deliver and showcase case teaching and its case collection to a global executive audience.

INSEAD Publishing, France, Singapore, United Arab Emirates, USA
https://publishing.insead.edu/
INSEAD has a longstanding reputation for producing high-quality, bestselling, award-winning cases of all types. INSEAD features frequently in the global bestselling lists for

its cases across many disciplines, and more recently has pioneered the development of integrated case learning with virtual reality as part of their experimental, immersive, innovative learning initiative.

Ivey Publishing, Richard Ivey Business School, Canada

www.iveycases.com/

Ivey Publishing holds a vast database of case studies and teaching notes produced by faculty from the Richard Ivey Business School since 1923 as well as from external case writers. Ivey Publishing also holds a number of other case collections, for which it has distributing rights. These collections include Harvard and Darden, as well as other collections from China, Singapore, South Africa and India. Individual authors can submit cases to Ivey, and if accepted then the author is paid royalties on any sales and the copyright for the case remains with Ivey. They also produce training materials and textbooks on the Ivey case method as well as running workshops for case teachers and case writers.

North American Case Research Association (NACRA), USA

www.nacra.net/

NACRA is a membership-based organisation which brings together hundreds of case writers, researchers and tutors to support the case development process. They are responsible for the *Case Research Journal* (CRJ) and a regular case newsletter, they provide fellowships and competitions and host an annual conference. They are affiliated to a network of localised case research associations based across America, Canada, Mexico and the Caribbean.

Society for Case Research (SCR)

https://sfcr.org/

SCR originated in the USA as a membership-based organisation, established in 1978, to support case research, writing and teaching. SCR publishes three scholarly journals, the *Business Case Journal* (BCJ), *Journal of Case Studies* (JCS), and the *Journal of Critical Incidents* (JCI). SCR also hosts an annual conference and publishes its proceedings as well as a members' newsletter.
Network

The Future of Management Education (FOME) Alliance

www.fome.group/

Established in 2018, FOME is an alliance of global business schools, with a strong reputation for case-based learning, comprised of Imperial College Business School, ESMT Berlin, BI Norwegian Business School, the Lee Kong Chian School of Business at Singapore Management University, IE Business School, EDHEC Business School, University of Melbourne and Ivey Business School as a knowledge-sharing network looking to pioneer online learning.

References

Allison, G. and Zelikow, P. (2004) Explaining the Cuban Missile Crisis. In R. Yin (ed.), *The Case Study Anthology*. Newbury Park, CA: Sage Publications, pp13–24.

Anderson, P. A. (1983) Decision Making by Objection and the Cuban Missile Crisis. *Administrative Science Quarterly*, 28(2), pp201–222.

Andrews, S. (2015) *A Critical and Theological Examination of Attitudes and Behaviours towards Mission, Leadership and Organisational Structures in Large Growing Churches in the UK*. Bristol: University of Bristol.

Andrews, S. (2021) *The Case Study Companion: Teaching, Learning and Writing Business Case Studies*. Abingdon: Routledge.

Baxter, P., and Jack, S. (2008) Qualitative Case Study Methodology: Study Design and Implementation for Novice Researchers. *The Qualitative Report*, 13(4), pp544–556.

Benbaum-Fich, R., Hiltz, R. S., and Turoff, M. (2001) A Comparative Content Analysis of Face-to-Face vs. ALN-Mediated Teamwork. In *Proceedings of the 34th Hawaii International Conference on Systems Sciences*, pp1–10.

Bennett, A., and Elman, C. (2010) Case Study Methods. In C. Reus-Smit and D. Snidal (eds) *The Oxford Handbook of International Relations*. Oxford: Oxford University Press, pp170–195.

Bitsch, V. (2005) Qualitative Research: A Grounded Theory Example and Evaluation Criteria. *Journal of Agribusiness*, 23(1), pp75–91.

Bixler, A., Eslinger, M., Kleinschmit, A. J., Gaudier-Diaz, M. M., Sankar, U., Marsteller, P., Goller, C. C., and Robertson, S. (2021) Three Steps to Adapt Case Studies for Synchronous and Asynchronous Online Learning. *Journal of Microbiology and Biology Education*, 22(1), pp1–4.

Blatter, J., and Blume, T. (2008) In Search of Co-variance, Causal Mechanisms or Congruence? Towards a Plural Understanding of Case Studies. *Swiss Political Science Review*, 14(2), pp315–356.

Brady, H., and Collier, D. (2004) *Rethinking Social Inquiry: Diverse Tools, Shared Standards*. Lanham: Rowman and Littlefield.

Bressanelli, G., Perona, M., and Saccani, N. (2019) Challenges in Supply Chain Redesign for the Circular Economy: A Literature Review and a Multiple Case Study. *International Journal of Production Research*, 57(23), pp7395–7422.

Bryman, A. (1989) *Research Methods and Organisation Studies* (Contemporary Social Research Series 20). London: Unwin Hyman Ltd.

Bryman, A. (2004) *Social Research Methods* (2nd edn). Oxford: Oxford University Press.

Bryman, A. (2015) *Social Research Methods* (5th edn). Oxford: Oxford University Press.

Burawoy, M. (1979) *Manufacturing Consent*. Chicago: University of Chicago Press.

Cavendish, R. (1982) *Women on the Line*. London: Routledge & Kegan Paul.

Charlebois, S., and Foti, L. (2017) Using a Live Case Study and Co-opetition to Explore Sustainability and Ethics in a Classroom: Exporting Fresh Water to China. *Global Business Review*, 18(6), pp1400–1411.

Cranston, N. (2008) The Use of Cases in the Leadership Development of Principals: A Recent Initiative in One Large Education System in Australia. *Journal of Educational Administration*, 46(5), pp581–597.

Creswell, J. W., and Poth, C. N. (2017) *Qualitative Inquiry and Research Design: Choosing Among Five Approaches* (4th edn). Newbury Park, CA: Sage Publications.

Culpin, V., and Scott, H. (2012) The Effectiveness of a Live Case Study Approach: Increasing Knowledge and Understanding of 'Hard' versus 'Soft' Skills in Executive Education. *Management Learning*, 43(5), pp565–577.

Denzin, N. K., and Lincoln, Y. S. (2018) *The Sage Handbook of Qualitative Research* (5th edn). Newbury Park, CA: Sage Publications.

Edmondson, A. C., Bohmer, R. M., and Pisano, G. P. (2001) Disrupted Routines: Team Learning and New Technology Implementation in Hospitals. *Administrative Science Quarterly*, 46(4), pp685–716.

Eisenhardt, K. M. (1989) Building Theories from Case Study Research. *Academy of Management Review*, 14(4), pp532–550.

Eisenhardt, K. M., and Graebner, M. E. (2007) Theory Building from Cases: Opportunities and Challenges. *Academy of Management Journal*, 50(1), pp25–32.

Elam, E. L. R., and Spotts, H. E. (2004) Achieving Marketing Curriculum Integration: A Live Case Study Approach. *Journal of Marketing Education*, 26(1), pp50–65.

Ellet, W. (2018) *The Case Study Handbook* (Revised Edition). Boston: Harvard Business School Press.

Erskine, J. A., Leenders, M. R., and Mauffette-Leenders, L. A. (2003) *Teaching with Cases* (3rd edn.). Canada: Ivey Publishing.

Farhoomand, A. (2004) Writing Teaching Cases: A Quick Reference Guide. *Communications of the Association for Information Systems*, 13, pp103–107. Available at: www.acrc.hku.hk/Content/Document/case.writing.guide.pdf (accessed 3 May 2023).

Fisher, I., and Ziviani, J. (2004) Explanatory Case Studies: Implications and Applications for Clinical Research. *Australian Occupational Therapy Journal*, 51, pp185–191.

Gabaldón, P. (2020) *Tips to Go Online During Covid-19 Crisis*. Available at: https://iepublishing.ie.edu/en/news/post/tips-to-go-online-during-covid-19-crisis (accessed 3 May 2023).

Galunic, D. C., and Eisenhardt, K. M. (2001) Architectural Innovation and Modular Corporate Forms. *The Academy of Management Journal*, 44(6), pp1229–1249.

Gerring, J. (2004) What is a Case Study and What Is It Good for? *American Political Science Review*, 98(2), pp341–354.

Gilbert, C. G. (2005) Unbundling the Structure of Inertia: Resource versus Routine Rigidity. *The Academy of Management Journal*, 48(5), pp741–763.

Gladwell, M. (2009) *Outliers: The Story of Success*. London: Penguin Books.

Gomm, R., Hammersley, M., and Foster, P. (2000) *Case Study Method*. Newbury Park, CA: Sage Publications Ltd.

Gratton, M. F., and O'Donnell, S. (2011) Communication Technologies for Focus Groups with Remote Communities: A Case Study of Research with First Nations in Canada. *Qualitative Research*, 11(2), pp159–175.

Green, A., and Erdem, M. (2016) Bridging the Gap Between Academic and Industry in Hospitality: Using Real Life Case Studies. *Developments in Business Simulation and Experiential Learning*, 43, pp43–46.

Guba, E. G., and Lincoln, Y. S. (1989) *Fourth Generation Evaluation*. Newbury Park, CA: Sage Publications.

Gustafsson, J. (2017) *Single Case Studies vs. Multiple Case Studies: A Comparative Study*. Academy of Business, Engineering and Science, Halmstad University, Sweden. Available at: www.diva-portal.org/smash/get/diva2:1064378/FULLTEXT01.pdf (accessed 3 May 2023).

Hammond, J. S. (2002) *Learning by the Case Method*. Boston: Harvard Business School Press.

Heath, J. (2015) *Teaching and Writing Case Studies: A Practical Guide* (4th edn). Cranfield: The Case Centre.

Heckman, R., and Annabi, H. (2005) A Content Analytic Comparison of Learning Processes in Online and Face-to-Face Case Study Discussions. *Journal of Computer-Mediated Communication*, 10(2), JCMC10210.

Ivey Publishing (2020) *10 Tips for Taking Case Classes Online*. Available at: www.iveycases.com/News/10-tips-for-taking-case-classes-online (accessed 3 May 2023).

Johnson, G. M., and Buck, G. H. (2007) *Asynchronous and Synchronous Online Discussion: Real and Perceived Achievement Differences*. Paper presented to the Annual Conference of the American Educational Research Association. April 2007, Chicago, IL. Available at: https://files.eric.ed.gov/fulltext/ED496130.pdf (accessed 3 May 2023).

Johnson, G., and Scholes, K. (1993) *Exploring Corporate Strategy* (3rd edn). Hoboken, NJ: Prentice Hall International.

Keller, K. (2013) *Strategic Brand Management: Building, Measuring and Managing Brand Equity* (4rd edn). New York: Pearson.

Kidder, T. (1982) *Soul of a New Machine*. New York: Avon.

Kolb, D. A. (2014) *Experiential Learning: Experience as the Source of Learning and Development* (2nd edn). New Jersey: Pearson Education.

Kotler, P., and Keller, K. (2008) *Marketing Management International Version* (13th edn). New Jersey: Pearson Education.

Kupp, M., and Mueller, U. (2020) Moving Case Teaching Online Quickly: Shared Experiences. Available at: https://youtu.be/7JIniWDf7uo (accessed 3 May 2023).

Kyei-Blankson, L., Godwyll, F., and Nur-Awaleh, M. A. (2014) Innovative Blended Delivery and Learning: Exploring Student Choice, Experience, and Level of Satisfaction in a Hyflex Course. *International Journal of Innovation and Learning*, 16(3), p243.

Lambert, C., and Sponem, S. (2012) Roles, Authority and Involvement of the Management Accounting Function: A Multiple Case-study Perspective, *European Accounting Review*, 21(3), pp565–589.

Lee, A. (2020) *Moving Case Teaching Online Quickly: Best Practice*. Available at: https://youtu.be/VgJDU4E38T4 (accessed 3 May 2023).

Liu, J., Socrate, S., and Pacheco, J. (2020) *Guide to Transitioning to Remote Teaching (Part I)*. Available at: https://meche.mit.edu/meche-virtual-resources/educational-resources-teaching-assistants#slides (accessed 3 May 2023).

Mairing, J. P., Sidabutar, R., Lada, E. Y., and Aritonang, H. (2021) Synchronous and Asynchronous Online Learning of Advanced Statistics During Covid-19 Pandemic. *Journal of Research and Advances in Mathematics Education*, 6(3), pp191–205.

Mauffette-Leenders, L. A., Erskine, J. A., and Leenders, M. R. (2007) *Learning with Cases* (4th edn). Canada: Ivey Publishing.

May, T. (2011) *Social Research: Issues, Methods and Process*. Maidenhead: Open University Press.

McNair, M. P. (1971) *McNair on Cases*. Boston: Harvard Business School Bulletin.

Mills, A. J., Durepos, G., and Wiebe, E. (2010) *Encyclopedia of Case Study Research*. Newbury Park, CA: Sage Publications.

Mintzberg, H., and Waters, J. A. (1982) Tracking Strategy in an Entrepreneurial Firm. *Academy of Management Journal*, 25(3), p465.

Morgan, D. L. (1988) *Focus Groups as Qualitative Research*. London: Sage.

Morris, R. J. (2022) *The Ultimate Guide to Compact Cases: Case Research, Writing, and Teaching*. Bingley: Emerald Publishing Ltd.

Morse, K. (2003) Does One Size Fit All? Exploring Asynchronous Learning in a Multicultural Environment. *Journal of Asynchronous Learning Networks*, 7(1), pp37–55.

Muilenburg, L. Y., and Berge, Z. L. (2005) Student Barriers to Online Learning: A Factor Analytic Study. *Journal of Distance Education*, 26(1), pp29–48.

Pappas, C. (2019) *Six Unexpected Uses of Case Studies in Online Training*. Available at: www.efrontlearn ing.com/blog/2019/08/unexpected-uses-case-studies-online-training.html (accessed 3 May 2023).

Patton, M. Q. (2002) *Qualitative Research and Evaluation Methods* (3rd edn). Newbury Park, CA: Sage Publications.

Pettigrew, A. (1985) *The Awakening Giant: Continuity and Change in Imperial Chemical Industries.* Oxford: Blackwell.

Pinfield, L. T. (1986) A Field Evaluation of Perspectives on Organizational Decision Making. *Administrative Science Quarterly*, 31(3), pp365–388.

Pollert, A. (1981) *Girls, Wives, Factory Lives.* London: Macmillan.

Ragin, C. C., and Becker, H. S. (1992) *What is a Case? Exploring the Foundations of Social Inquiry.* Cambridge: Cambridge University Press.

Rapp, A., and Ogilvie, J. (2019) *Live Case Studies Demystified*. Available at: https://hbsp.harvard.edu/ inspiring-minds/live-case-studies-demystified (accessed 3 May 2023).

Raufflet, E., and Mills, A. J. (2017) *The Dark Side: Critical Cases in the Downside of Business.* Abingdon: Routledge.

Reinhardt, R., Gurtner, S., and Griffin, A. (2018) Towards an Adaptive Framework of Low-end Innovation Capability: A Systematic Review and Multiple Case Study Analysis. *Long Range Planning*, 51(5), pp770–796.

Rosenbaum-Elliott, R., Percy, L., and Pervan, S. (2015) Strategic Brand Management (3rd edn). New York: Oxford University Press.

Saunders, M., Lewis, P., and Thornhill, A. (2016) *Research Methods for Business Students* (7th edn). Harlow: Pearson Education.

Schiano, B., and Andersen, E. (2017) *Teaching with Cases Online*. Boston: Harvard Business Publishing. Available at: https://s3.amazonaws.com/he-product-images/docs/Article_Teaching_With_Cases_ Online.pdf (accessed 3 May 2023).

Schonell, S. and Macklin, R. (2019) Work Integrated Learning Initiatives: Live Case Studies as a Mainstream WIL Assessment. *Studies in Higher Education*, 44(7), pp1197–1208.

Seale, C. (2006) Generating Grounded Theory. In C. Seale (ed.), *Researching Society and Culture* (2nd edn). Oxford: Sage Publications.

Seaton, J. X., and Schwier, R. (2014) An Exploratory Case Study of Online Instructors: Factors Associated with Instructor Engagement. *International Journal of E-Learning & Distance Education*, 29(1), pp1–16. Available at: http://ijede.ca/index.php/jde/article/view/870/1536 (accessed 3 May 2023).

Seethamraju, R. (2014) Effectiveness of Using Online Discussion Forum for Case Study Analysis. *Education Research International*, ID 589860.

Shapiro, B. P. (1984) *Hints for Case Teaching*. Boston: Harvard Business Publishing.

Simmons, E. (2013) *Learning with Cases: What's Involved?* The Case Centre. Available at: www.thecas ecentre.org/caseMethod/features/learningwithcases (accessed 3 May 2023).

Simmons, E. (2019) *Preparing Students to Learn with Cases*. The Case Centre. Available at: www.thecas ecentre.org/caseMethod/features/preparingStudents (accessed 3 May 2023).

Simons, H. (2009) *Case Study Research in Practice*. London: Sage Productions Ltd.

Sklar, J. (2020) 'Zoom Fatigue' is Taxing the Brain. Here's Why That Happens. *National Geographic.* Available at: www.nationalgeographic.com/science/2020/04/coronavirus-zoom-fatigue-is-taxing-the-brain-here-is-why-that-happens/ (accessed 3 May 2023).

Stake, R. E. (1995) *The Art of Case Study Research*. Newbury Park, CA: Sage Publications.

Stake, R. E. (2000) The Case Study Method in Social Enquiry. In R. Gomm, M. Hammersley, and P. Foster (eds), *Case Study Method*. Newbury Park, CA: Sage Publications.

Stern, E., Stame, N., Mayne, J., Forss, K., Davies, R., and Befani, B. (2012) *Broadening the Range of Designs and Methods for Impact Evaluations*. Report of a study commissioned by the Department for International Development (DFID). Working paper 38, April 2012.

Thomas, G. (2021) *How To Do Your Case Study* (3rd edn). London: Sage Publications.

Toulmin, S. E. (2003) *The Uses of Argument* (Updated Edition). Cambridge: Cambridge University Press.

USAID (2013) Evaluative Case Studies: Technical Note. Version 1, November 2013. US Bureau for Policy, Planning and Learning. Available at: https://usaidlearninglab.org/resources/technical-note-evaluative-case-studies (accessed 3 May 2023).

Valenta, A., Therriault, D., Dieter, M., and Mrtek, R. (2001) Identifying Student Attitudes and Learning Styles in Distance Education. *Journal of Asynchronous Learning Networks*, 5(2), pp111–127.

Van der Ham, V. (2016) *Analysing a Case Study*. New York: Palgrave Macmillan.

Varkey, T. C., Varkey, J. A., Ding, J. B., Varkey, P. K., Zeitler, C., Nguyen, A. M., Merhavy, Z. I., and Thomas, C. R. (2023) Asynchronous Learning: A General Review of Best Practices for the 21st Century, *Journal of Research in Innovative Teaching and Learning*, 16(1), pp4–16.

Wegerif, R. (2019) The Social Dimension of Asynchronous Learning Networks. *Online Learning*, 2(1), pp34–47.

Willis, B. (2014) *The Advantages and Limitations of Single Case Study Analysis*. E-International Relations. Available at: www.e-ir.info/2014/07/05/the-advantages-and-limitations-of-single-case-study-analysis/ (accessed 3 May 2023).

Wood, J. D. M., Leenders, M. R., Mauffette-Leenders, L. A., and Erskine, J. A. (2019) *Writing Cases* (5th edn). Canada: Leenders and Associates Inc.

Yelland, J., and Gifford, S. M. (1995) Problems of Focus Group Methods in Cross-cultural Research: A Case Study of Beliefs about Sudden Infant Death Syndrome. *Australian and New Zealand Journal of Public Health*, 19(3), pp257–263.

Yin, R. K. (1993) *Case Study Research: Design and Methods* (3rd edn). London: Sage Publications.

Yin, R. K. (2004) *The Case Study Anthology*. Newbury Park, CA: Sage Publications.

Yin, R. K. (2009) *Case Study Research: Design and Methods* (4th edn). London: Sage Publications.

Yin, R. K. (2018) *Case Study Research and Applications: Design and Methods* (6th edn). Newbury Park, CA: Sage Publications.

Index

Printed in the United States
by Baker & Taylor Publisher Services